Welcome to
WEAVING

The Modern Guide

Lindsey Campbell

Schiffer
Publishing Ltd

4880 Lower Valley Road • Atglen, PA 19310

hello hydrangea

Designed by Danielle D. Farmer
Cover design by Danielle D. Farmer
Type set in Silver South Script/Playfair Display/Merriweather/DIN-Light

ISBN: 978-0-7643-5631-5
Printed in China

Published by Schiffer Publishing, Ltd.
4880 Lower Valley Road
Atglen, PA 19310
Phone: (610) 593-1777; Fax: (610) 593-2002
E-mail: Info@schifferbooks.com
Web: www.schifferbooks.com

For our complete selection of fine books on this and related subjects, please visit our website at www.schifferbooks.com. You may also write for a free catalog.

Schiffer Publishing's titles are available at special discounts for bulk purchases for sales promotions or premiums. Special editions, including personalized covers, corporate imprints, and excerpts, can be created in large quantities for special needs. For more information, contact the publisher.

We are always looking for people to write books on new and related subjects. If you have an idea for a book, please contact us at proposals@schifferbooks.com.

Other Schiffer Books on Related Subjects:

The Art of Weaving a Life: A Framework to Expand and Strengthen Your Personal Vision, Susan Barrett Merrill, ISBN 978-0-7643-5264-5

Weaving Patterned Bands: How to Create and Design with 5, 7, and 9 Pattern Threads, Susan J. Foulkes, ISBN 978-0-7643-5550-9

Inspiration Kantha: Creative Stitchery and Quilting with Asia's Ancient Technique, Anna Hergert, ISBN 978-0-7643-5357-4

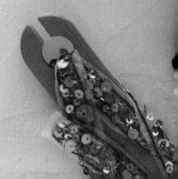

To my mom,
who encouraged me to make
creative messes as a little girl.

To my husband,
who encourages me to make
creative messes as a woman.

Contents

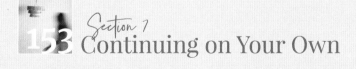

Introduction

My love for fiber arts began at a young age. In fact, it began when I was ten years old and my grandfather died. I would ride my bike to my grandma's house every week to spend the afternoon with her as she taught me how to crochet. She would hold the fingers of my left hand in place, *just so*, and I would crochet unmeasurable lengths of single-chain stitches while we sat together. I loved watching her hands work furiously next to me as she completed her own projects in record speed.

Although I grew apart from crochet, I continued to pursue fine arts throughout high school and college, becoming interested in jewelry design, illustration, photography, graphic design, and ceramics, to name a few. Each new medium built upon the skills I had learned before, and I was hungry to learn more about each new approach to the visual arts. I began a small, personal craft/life blog to document my interests called Hello Hydrangea while taking a floral-design class.

When I graduated from Brigham Young University with my BA in advertising and visual arts, my husband was offered a great job in a new region of the country, far away from most of our friends and family. During those first few weeks alone in our new home, as I continued my own job search, I felt the pull of my forgotten crochet supplies and decided to learn yet another medium. Although I had few resources, and certainly no teacher for weaving, I made a loom out of an old picture frame and taught myself through vintage pamphlets and shaky YouTube videos. I was

completely hooked after the first piece, even though it began to fall apart as soon as I cut it off the loom. I continued to teach myself and share my designs as the years passed, during spare hours before and after my successful career as a marketing design director. I have been weaving almost every day since.

I love weaving, more than I can express. I love the slow process. I love the search for the perfect yarn. I love the meditative properties it has on a busy mind. I love the respect it teaches for traditional practices that are still done today. I love the push and pull that are needed for proper tension. I love that even though I have completed hundreds of pieces, I learn something new every time I sit down at my loom. I dream about weaving, I really do! I also love the community that I have found through weaving.

I love teaching others how to weave because it means when I'm not actually weaving, I get to talk about weaving with others! I have taught thousands of students either in person or through my online weaving video classes. I've found that they always come back when they have caught the "weaver fever" and want to learn more! Through my Facebook group (Welcome to Weaving) they can do just that, by supporting, asking questions, and sharing their interest with thousands of fellow weavers.

Weaving has taught me that sometimes goals progress slowly. It has helped me learn patience as I eventually became a mother. It has taught me plenty of hard lessons. One of these is that sometimes hours of subpar work must be cut off and redone correctly. I remember this lesson when the balance of life tips too far one way or another, and I have to step back to reevaluate the whole picture and mend mistakes before they get too far. I imagine weaving as a friend that I go to on the good days and on the bad, to reflect inwardly and silently express myself.

I wrote this book to introduce you to my friend, weaving. Here you will find no judgment. I promise that you will catch the "weaver fever," just as I did years ago. The process will beckon you in, row by row, to create beautiful things. As you spend time at the loom I hope you appreciate the meditative practices that will allow your thoughts to grow, wander, and work through questions both in life and your design. If you enjoy being curious, challenged, and proud, then weaving is for you.

Welcome to weaving!

Lindsey

How to Use This Book

This book was created to go beyond being an introduction to weaving and to provide a reference guide as your skills grow. There are now many tutorials, blog posts, and videos available online for beginners who want to dip into the medium; learn the easiest, fastest way to weave; and then move on to something else. This book was intentionally created with a different purpose in mind. Here you will learn all the beginner terms and techniques, but with a deeper explanation of the best tips and tricks to continue to build your knowledge. Although you are welcome to jump around between chapters, this book is mapped out to reflect the process we go through when learning a new skill.

First, your interest is piqued when you see another artist's art piece and think, "I would love to learn how to do that."

Second, you begin searching for the tools you will need. You don't want to spend too much money on it before you decide if you enjoy the new skill, but you want something that will allow you to learn and grow.

Third, you find resources to teach you the basic techniques to get started.

Fourth, you feel confident in the basics and want to learn what other techniques are available to challenge the basic skills you have learned.

Fifth, you are ready to put all the techniques you have been practicing together by following a premade design, or copying an existing design in a project. You may complete one and then try again with a different design, continuing to refer back to the techniques you learned as you practice them on projects.

And finally, you feel confident in what you have learned and ready to venture outside the premade designs to find your own style. You may try an unconventional approach to the skill or create a project beyond a sampler.

This is the common approach to the process of learning a craft, the stages that each person works through. Each chapter in this book covers a new step. You are welcome to follow along from start to finish for an intensive, comprehensive lesson in weaving, or to skip around.

In the project gallery on the next page, you will find inspiration by looking over the completed design for each project included in this book.

Section 1 covers the materials and tools you will need for weaving. You will begin to build your vocabulary as you understand common weaving terms. You'll find a tutorial for making your first frame loom, along with a breakdown of different yarns and tools. You can begin gathering your supplies to weave.

Section 2 covers the basics of weaving that you will need to know. This includes setting up a loom, removing a tapestry, how to keep your tension even, and tips for quicker weaving. These tips and tricks are important to learn from the very beginning to save you from a lot of heartache as you continue your weaving journey.

Section 3 introduces a small group of beginner techniques, with which you can create almost any design you have in mind. Each technique includes a list of the projects that use it later on in the book, so that once you learn the technique you can refer to the projects to see it in action on a full-scale tapestry.

Section 4 includes more-challenging techniques to have fun with. Again, each technique includes a list of projects that use it later on in the book and that will expand your creativity as you think outside the box with these methods.

Section 5 covers 7 tapestry projects. The most common way to use modern weaving is by creating a tapestry to display your work. Each tapestry has a theme and refers back to any techniques that are used, so that you can revisit them if you need to. Some tapestries are more difficult, but each one can be re-created by a beginner weaver.

Section 6 is the most advanced part of this book. It begins with projects that you can create from tapestries, such as necklaces or bags. These projects include a general explanation on how to manipulate the resources that you have into a usable project. Although the designs for each project are not explained in as much detail as in Section 5, they are meant to be used as inspiration to take your own designs and follow the tutorials to create something unique.

Section 7 is a jumping-off point to explore weaving further, outside the book, as you continue to develop your own style.

The techniques and projects in this book will set you up to be able to weave anything you have in mind. I created this book as a tool that you can refer back to again and again. The techniques and projects will continue to answer your projects' needs in different ways as your weaving skills progress. Keep it close to your loom to open up when you want to follow a specific method or just to find inspiration if you are faced with a creative block. There is something for everyone, no matter what your weaving style is!

Learn to Make . . .

Need some inspiration to get you started? Here are the exact tapestries and projects you will learn how to create later on in the book. You can jump ahead to follow each one's step-by-step instructions, or continue reading to learn about specific techniques and terms beforehand.

Page 116

Page 128

Page 140

Page 119

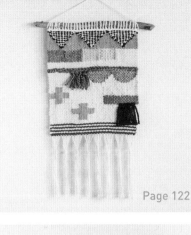

Page 122

Page 125

Page 131

Page 134

Page 138

Page 141

Page 142

Page 144

Page 146

Page 148

Page 150

Section 1
MATERIALS

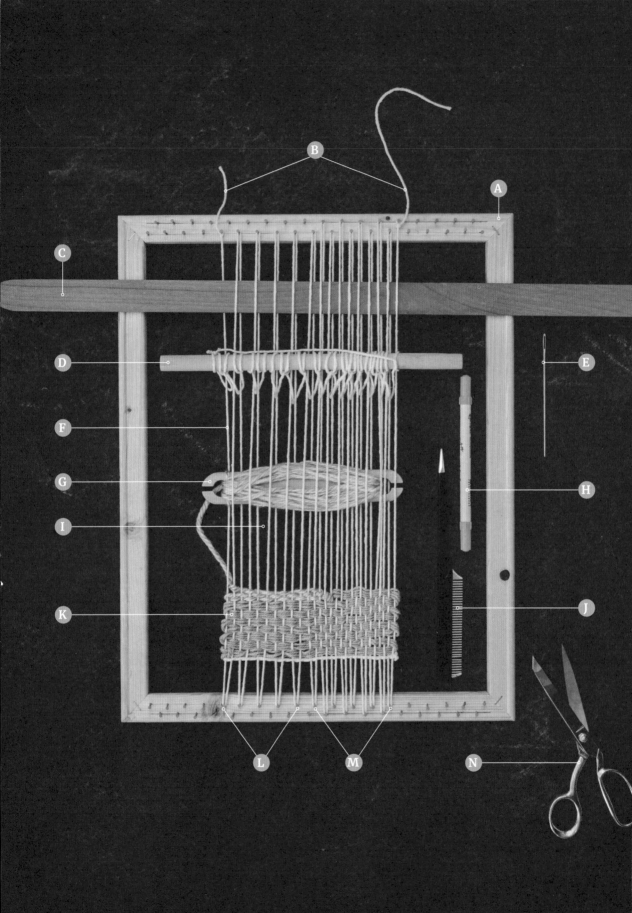

Anatomy of a Loom

A Frame loom. A simple loom involving pegs/notches on polar ends of a frame to hold the vertical warp strings taut.

B Warp knotted on top. Begin and end your warp on the side of the loom farthest away from you.

C Sword. Also known as a pick-up stick or batten, this is used to lift half of the warp strings and open the shed.

D Heddle. Device used for faster weaving. Lifts the other half of the warp strings to open the warp shed, so that the shuttle can quickly pass through.

E Tapestry needle. A long, smooth needle with a large eye, used to tuck in tails and weave details.

F Warp. Strings held taut, vertically, across the loom.

G Shuttle. A tool that guides the weft through the shed.

H Felt tip marker. Used to draw outlines onto the warp.

I Warp shed. The space created between warp strings when some are lifted up for the shuttle to pass through to create rows of weft.

J Beater comb. A tool with teeth that is used to push rows of weft in place.

K Weft. Yarn guided through the shed to create horizontal rows.

L Low-density warp. Warp is more spread out, with fewer warp strings per inch. Used for looser, quicker weaving.

M High-density warp. Warp is closer together, with more warp strings per inch. Used for tighter, detailed weaving.

N Scissors.

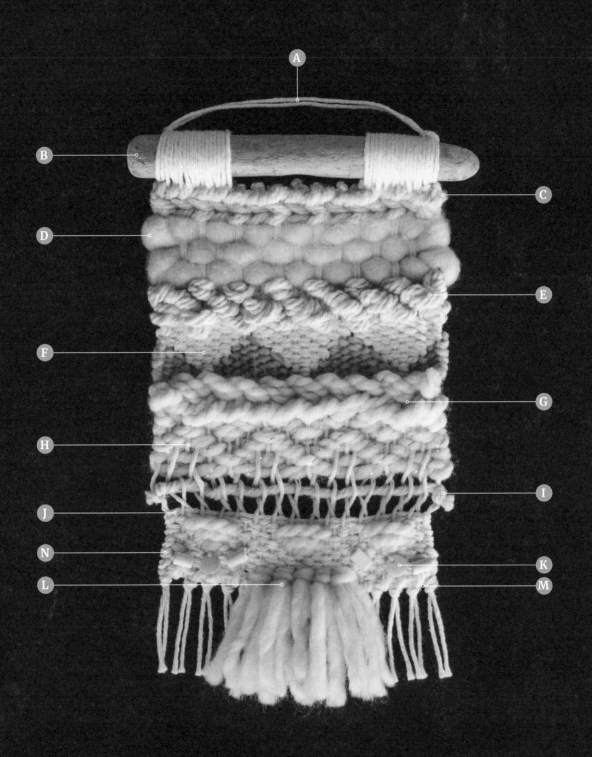

Anatomy of a Tapestry

(A) Hanger. A piece of string attached to the rod for easy hanging.

(B) Rod. A straight item to hang the tapestry from, usually 1–2" wider than the width of the tapestry.

(C) Twining header. The first row used to hold the following rows in place.

(D) Plain tabby weave. The basic plain weave; alternately goes over and under the warp strings.

(E) Pile weave. Loops created during tabby weave that extend beyond the surface of the tapestry.

(F) Shapes. Edges created from stairsteps as the weft rows pass over the warp strings.

(G) Soumak. A technique to create looped braiding effect.

(H) Twill. As rows of weft are added, the exposed warp strings create patterns.

(I) Leno. When a weft string holds manipulated warp strings in place.

(J) Supplementary weft. An additional weft that floats behind regular tabby rows and comes to the surface of the tapestry only to create patterns.

(K) Embellishments. Beads, tassels, baubles, and extra items that are added to the surface of the tapestry.

(L) Rya. A technique to create fringe and texture.

(M) Hem stitch. The last row used to hold the previous rows in place.

(N) Selvedge. The last few warp strings on either side of a tapestry.

Materials

Tapestries can be woven with almost any type of yarn you find! Each one will add its own personality as you weave, so practice with many kinds and soon you will understand which fibers you enjoy working with . . . and which ones you will avoid, depending on your style.

Warp yarns

Warp yarns are more of a tool than a yarn. The material you use for your warp can set you up for weaving success or failure. Your warp will be stretched, tightened, moved, strummed, and combed and needs to hold the weight of your weft when it is cut off the loom. That's a tall order for some thin string! With all that

your warp is put through, it needs to be strong and durable with a slight give so that you can pull open your shed without breaking any strings. It also needs to be tightly twisted to withstand the friction as weft rows are beaten down. Warp also needs to be smooth so that your weft rows don't get caught on any unnecessary fibers.

The best warp is made out of cotton. You can choose if you want it thick or thin, but it shouldn't be too thin that it snaps like a thread, or too thick that it can't wrap around your notches. My favorite is undyed cotton crochet yarn, worsted weight. It is smooth, strong, and tightly spun—it crosses all of my Xs for the perfect warp!

Weft yarns

CHARACTER

Hand spun and dyed—yarns that are hand-made have an extra-special personality. They can also be custom dyed if you have a certain color in mind.

Thick or thin—you can work with yarns that are chunky or lightweight. The size doesn't matter, although it will take many more rows of thin yarn to make up the space that a thick yarn can quickly complete.

Loose or tight—unlike warp yarn, weft yarns can be spun to many tightnesses. However, keep in mind that extra-tight yarn without any give will pull on your tension more (so weave looser than you think you need), and loose yarns could rip due to some of the pressure that comes with the pushing and pulling that is expected during weaving. See a sample of yarn thicknesses on the next page.

Textured or smooth—experimenting with rough versus smooth yarns is one of my favorite techniques. Play with lots of textures and try combining them in the same weave.

MATERIALS

Cotton—best used for warp but also excellent for weft. Has the perfect tooth to stay in place as you build up many rows, and is very durable.

Wool—many different stages are available for weaving, from unspun roving to loosely spun yarn to tightly spun.

Roving—fiber that has been carded but not spun. Because the fibers are not spun, it shows dust and grime more easily over time. Always rip, never cut.

Acrylic blend—plasticky feel, slippery, but easy to find and cheap

Linen—strawlike feel; does not stretch as well as other fibers but can be packed firmly as a weft. Possible to use as warp, but again, it does not have as much give as cotton.

Plant-based yarn—hemp, bamboo, nettle. Each has its own personality, and they are fun to experiment with, but will more easily disintegrate over time.

Sari silk—torn strips of silk that have been sewn end to end to create a continuous length. Tends to be stiffer and bulging compared to spun yarn, but adds a unique style.

Novelty—made of an unexpected material such as gold leaf, beads, pom-poms, metallic plastic, etc.

COLORS

Unlimited. Go crazy!

SOURCING

Local craft stores. Support small by shopping at your local yarn stores. Often, they hold classes, invite local artists to teach and display their work, and sell materials grown and spun around their location in the local region. Specialty shops are usually run by employees who have a passion and knowledge for yarn and craft and can help answer questions. Also, be sure to check your local weaver's guild; some hold an annual donated yarn sale including handmade yarn spun from the students/teachers.

Retail craft stores. The easiest place to pick up some yarn because they are widely found and usually have a big selection, plus lots of other craft materials. Because the yarns are usually cheaper, these are great places to find different yarns to experiment with until you become accustomed to the materials you prefer to work with, and you are ready to find specialty versions available somewhere else. Retail brands are easy to find if you ever need to repurchase the exact same yarn later on. Read the material labels. You don't need to spend a lot of money to find high-quality yarns. There are durable options made from all types of materials (wool, cotton, and even acrylic). However, sometimes 100 percent acrylic yarn can feel extra plasticky, and it will affect the ease of your weaving as well as the quality of the finished product.

Etsy. When you can't find what you need at your local craft or retail store, the best place to search is Etsy. On their search site you can find almost any type of material, color, thickness, and tightness that you want. You can also search for "hand spun" or "hand dyed" to find yarn that is unique and made by a fellow artisan.

Local markets. Search out your local wool/ yarn or craft festival. There may be booths selling yarn, and you can meet and speak to the artist who created the material. It is a great way to add an extra story to your tapestry.

Other online retailers. Many specialty yarn shops don't sell their materials in brick-and-mortar locations; instead they have online shops. Sometimes it is difficult to tell from a computer screen what a yarn feels and looks like in person, so do your best to read reviews and understand what characteristics different weights/thicknesses/materials have, so that you can trust your knowledge when purchasing online.

Yarn weights are shown on the left from thin to thick.

Yarn materials are shown on the right.

Fine / Sock / Fingering Weight

Light / DK / Light Worsted Weight

Medium / Worsted Weight

Bulky / Chunky / Rug Weight

Super Bulky / Roving Weight

Chiffon / Ribbon

Pencil Roving

Unspun / Comb Top Roving

Fabric Trim

Rope

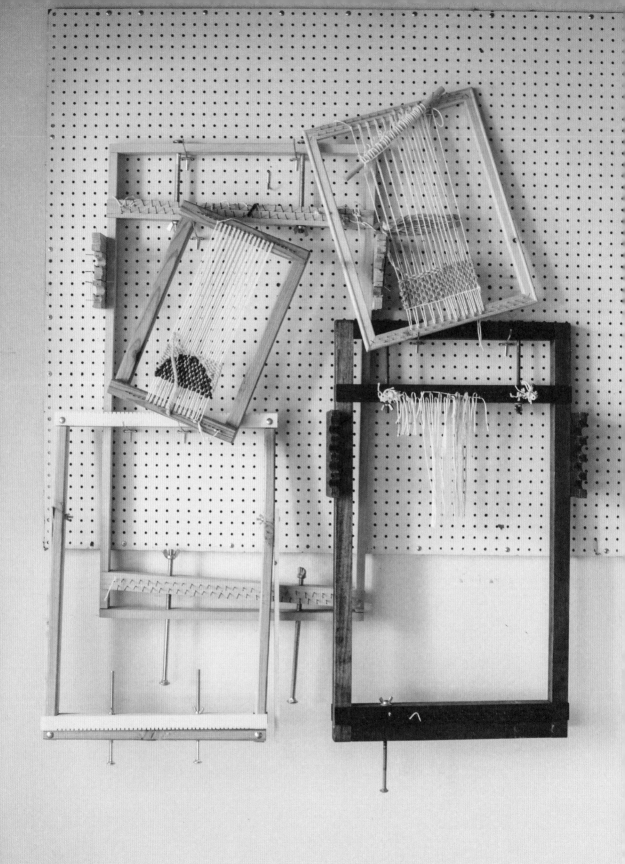

Looms

Every weaver's technique is slightly different, which is why there are so many different types of frame looms available. Looms come in all shapes and sizes, from portable I-shaped looms to giant looms. There are even looms that are circles or triangles or are made from unexpected items such as branches or hula hoops. Even standard rectangular looms have differences. Some are made with wood or plastic. Some have notches, pegs, or nails. Some are adjustable, and some have heddle stands. The secret is that whatever loom you happen to have, they all work the same as long as you can stretch your warp from one side to the other.

As a beginner you can learn on any loom you have available. It doesn't have to be expensive—some great looms even come from children's craft kits. There are many options for looms to invest in. As the size increases and the materials that are used increase in quality, so does the price for the loom. However, while a weaver may decide to upgrade the size of the loom to allow for larger projects or to add devices such as heddles to speed up their weaving, a loom does not determine a weaver's skill level. Many talented weavers still use a small basic loom.

THINGS TO CONSIDER WHEN BUYING A LOOM

Size. All looms work the same. They hold the warp strings tight. However, the only way a loom can limit your weaving ability is if the width of the warp doesn't reach the length you want. If you dream of making long tapestries to hang over your bed, a small loom will never be able to stretch any wider than it is made.

Durability. Even beginner looms need to be strong enough to hold your warp tightly. Most looms are made out of wood because it is straight and strong. You also want to make sure that your loom joins tightly at the corners, so that your frame stays true and square and won't lean to one side while you weave.

Features. There is no need to spend lots of money on a specially made stainless-steel loom with a solid gold stand. A loom's only job is to hold your warp tightly. No extra embellishments will help you become a better weaver. There are a few handy features such as adjustable bars or heddles or easel stands to consider, although they are unnecessary to learn how to weave.

Price. A beginner's loom shouldn't cost a lot. Truthfully, you can even use a cardboard box as a loom! However, if you find that you are truly enjoying the art of weaving and are willing to invest in a larger, more expensive loom, do your research, read reviews, and visit some local specialty stores to see them in person. A good loom will last a lifetime!

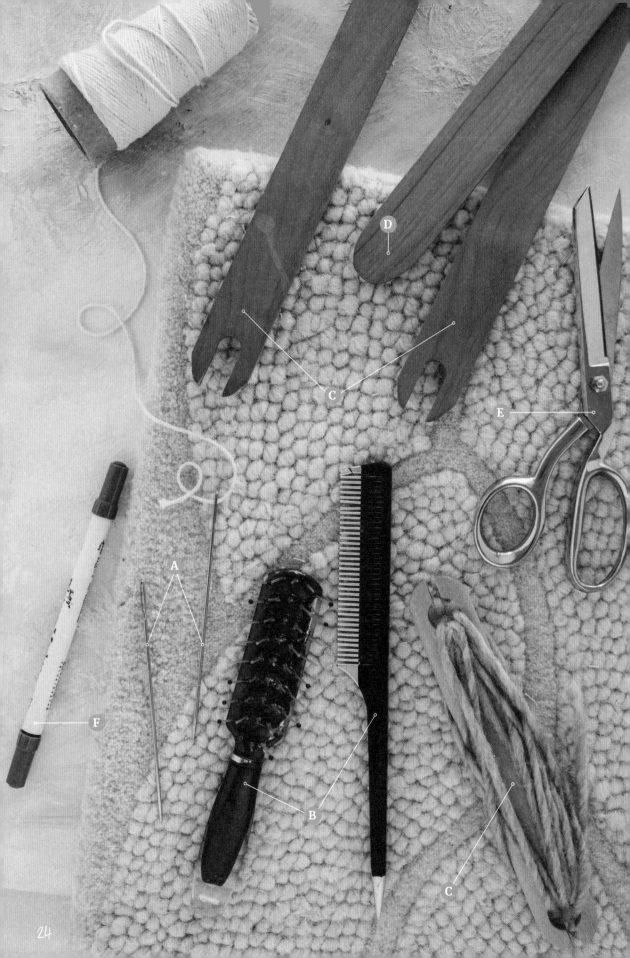

TOOLS

Although weaving is a simple craft that can be done with a simple loom and yarn, there are many tools that make the process easier and sometimes even faster.

Ⓐ Weaving needle—some weavers choose to use bobbins or shuttles to guide their weft through the warp sheds. While there are beautiful tools associated with weaving, I recommend using a weaving needle. They are about 5 inches long, straight, and made of metal, with a large eye for all thicknesses of yarn.

Ⓑ Beater—a regular comb, hairbrush, or even a fork are great tools to bat down your weft rows so that they are firmly stacked in place.

Ⓒ Shuttle—a long tool used to wrap weft material around, for continuous weaving without stopping to attach a new length. Best used for large sections woven with the same material.

Ⓓ Shed stick—a flat tool woven through the top of the weave to pick up a pattern of warp strings at the same time, so that the shuttle can easily pass through the open shed. Only one can be used at a time. Often partnered with a heddle so that the shuttle can easily pass through a full row.

Ⓔ Scissors—any scissors will do.

Ⓕ Fabric marker—used to draw designs onto your warp.

● Ruler (not pictured)—you will need to measure how many notches to include in your warp to achieve the desired length of your finished tapestry.

● Heddle (not pictured)—a device using fiber leashes to pick up a pattern of warp strings at the same time so that the shuttle can easily pass through the open shed. An unlimited number of heddles can be used for complex twill patterns.

RODS

Choosing a rod to hang your weaving or tapestry on is a great way to further your design. Get creative with what you hang your

finished tapestry on. Some great choices are dowels, natural sticks, metal piping, or driftwood. Most common hangers are straight because they are easier to attach to the edge of a tapestry. They should also extend 1–2 inches wider than your tapestry.

Smooth, straight sticks and dowels are easiest to use because you can simply slide the loops of your warp strings onto them. If your stick has extra personality in the form of a branch, curves, or different widths throughout, you will need to use the more advanced method of sewing on your tapestry.

If you want to use something other than wood, copper piping is a popular choice. The pipe will need to be cut using a pipe-cutting tool and then deburred and cleaned with a wire brush. The edges can be very sharp, so use caution.

Depending on your design, weaving projects don't have to be hung on straight rods alone. A circular hoop or recycled bag handle are also fun to experiment with. In the end, as long as you can sew your tapestry around an object, you can hang your design from it!

EMBELLISHMENTS

While yarn is the base overall material of choice for weaving tapestries, it is also fun to add extra embellishments of all kinds. These can be in the form of beads, charms, crystals or stones, trim, tassels, or sequins.

Incorporating a special embellishment not only adds personality to the design of your tapestry but allows you to enrich the meaning behind your display. You can find embellishments by going to a bead store or even taking apart jewelry. Search online for handmade, vintage, antique, bulk, or global jewelry pieces for extra-special items. You can read more about embellishments and how to incorporate them in your design later in the book.

Make a Loom

If you feel up to it, go ahead and make your first loom yourself! It is often a cheaper option and takes only three easy steps. I made my first loom because I couldn't find all the features I wanted combined in one design. It is still my favorite loom to weave with.

You can use many household items to create a usable loom. The key to success is finding a sturdy frame of some sort that won't buckle or lean when your warp is wrapped tightly between the edges.

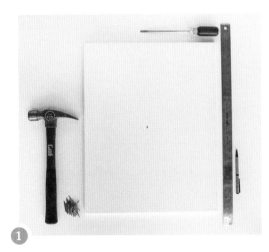

Gather supplies. You will need a stretched canvas (this one is 18" × 20"), a ruler, a pencil, a screwdriver, some finishing nails, and a hammer.

A large, cheap option is to use a canvas stretcher. You can pick one up at your local craft store. There are many different sizes to choose from, although many times they already have canvas stapled on the frame. Simply remove the canvas by picking out the staples in the back. If you are extra handy and possess woodworking tools, you can also make your own frame with a few pieces of wood and some screws. This gives you full control over the size of your loom. Just make sure that your edges are square.

(Step-by-step pictures on following page)

2 Use your screwdriver to dig out the staples that hold the canvas in place in the back.

3 Remove the wooden frame from the canvas.

4 Use a ruler to draw two parallel lines ¼"−1" apart on each of the farthest edges of your frame.

5 Use a ruler to mark points ⅓" apart, alternating between the two lines so that every other point is placed above and then below along the width of your frame.

Alternating the placement of the nails will make it easier to warp the loom later on and will keep the frame from cracking because too many nails are in one row.

6 Add nails. Use a hammer to pound a small nail into each mark, and then go back to lightly angle the nails on both sides of the loom away from each other. This added step helps hold the warp strings in place during any strenuous lifting or pulling while you weave.

7 Repeat on the far side of the frame so that the nails match up straight and your loom is complete. farthest edges of your frame.

Now you are ready to warp up your loom and start weaving!

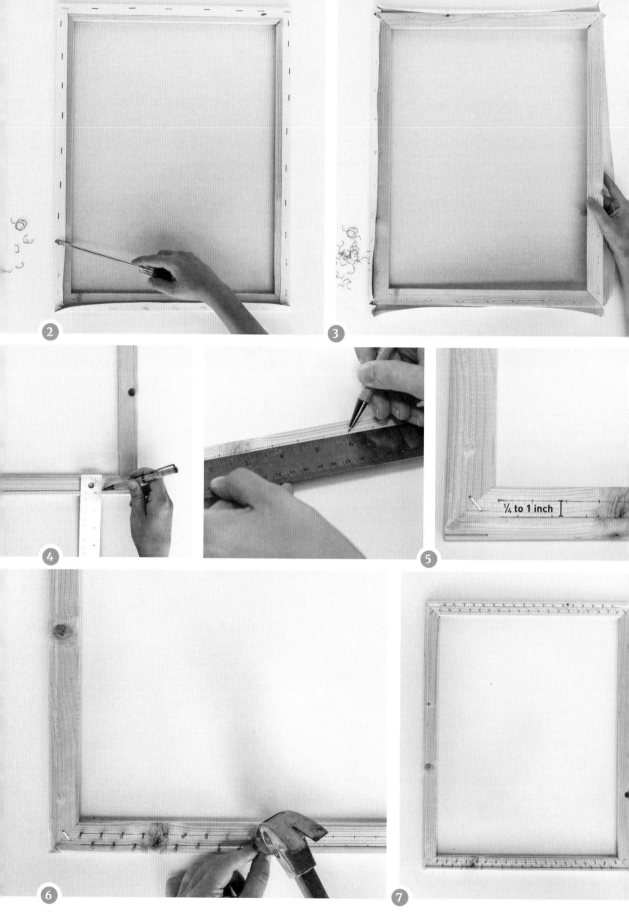

Preparing Shuttles

There are a few tools to guide your weft through your warp shed as you build up rows of your tapestry. My preferred tool of choice is the tapestry needle because it allows you to create details and be precise when it comes to interlocking, hatching, or tucking your ends down without changing tools.

If you plan on covering a large space with the same yarn, you can do this more quickly and with minimal knots in the back by using a different tool called a shuttle. The shuttle allows you to weave more continuously without stopping so often to attach more yarn when you run out. It also speeds up your process when combined with a heddle setup.

To use a shuttle, you must load it with yarn. Begin by holding a tail of yarn in the center of the forks on one side.

Wrap the yarn around the forks in a single figure eight to hold them in place.

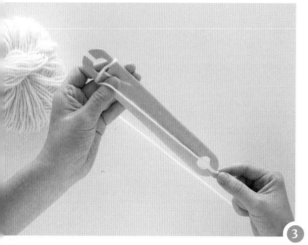

Pull the yarn down to the other side.

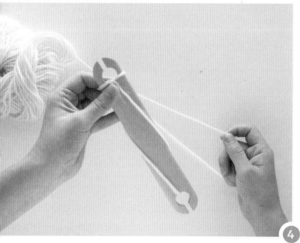

Wrap the yarn lengthwise around the shuttle in a figure-eight pattern around the outside edges to keep the bulk as flat and wide as possible, so that it will pass through the shed more easily.

Each time the yarn exits the fork at the top, wrap it down to the fork on the other side and around the back clockwise.

Section 2

PREPARATION

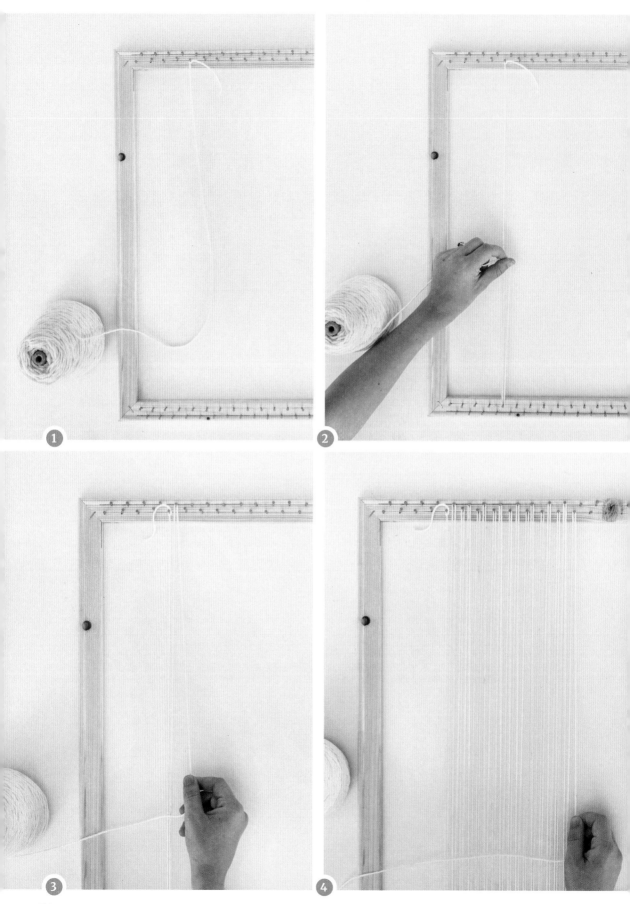

Warping

Planning

You do not need to premeasure your warp string. Simply pull string off the cone/ball as you go. If you have a specific space or rod you want the tapestry to fit, create a contained warp. Before warping, plan how wide you want your tapestry so that you can measure how many notches on your loom you need to use.

Choosing the correct warp string is important. It needs to be strong, a consistent thickness, hard twisted, smooth, and not too thick to withstand the constant tension and friction as you pass weft rows through and beat them into place. The best warp string is made from cotton.

Warp your loom while it is lying flat on the ground or a table. This will make it easier to maintain even tension as you pull the warp string back and forth across your loom. Begin and end with knots oriented on the top side of your loom (the side farthest away from you). This will always result in an even number of warp strings to work with, for easier hanging once you remove the tapestry from the loom.

1. Count the number of notches (nails) that you need to span your desired length, and center this number in the middle of your loom. I want my finished tapestry to be 10" wide, which comprises 20 notches on my loom. I find the center 20 notches and will have nine leftovers (unused notches) on either end. Take the end of your warp string and tie a knot around the top far-left notch that you will be using for your project.

2. Carry the thread down to the bottom of the loom to wrap it around the parallel notch on the other end. Be sure that each warp string is straight and not diagonal.

3. Carry the thread up to the top of the loom again to wrap it around the next notch and then back to the bottom.

4. Repeat these steps until you reach the last notch at the top of your loom.

5. Tie a knot and cut off the string.

Maintain even tension

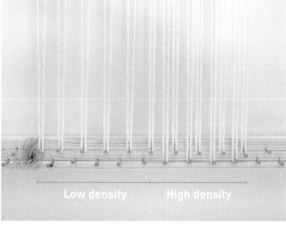

Low density   High density

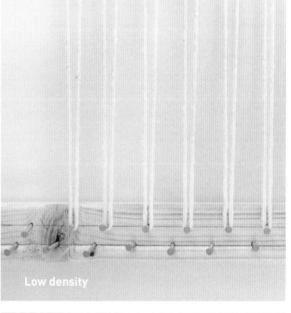

Low density

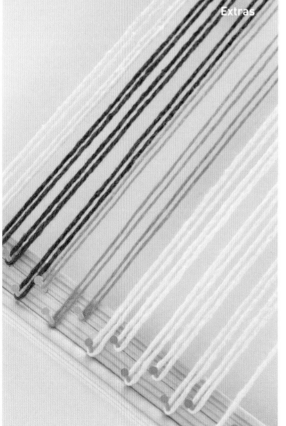

Extras

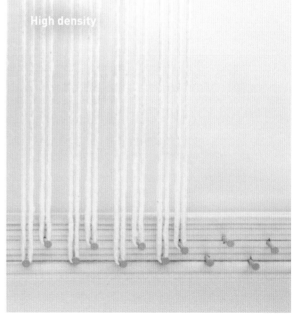

High density

MAINTAIN EVEN TENSION

The key to keeping good tension while warping is not to let go of the warp string as you are carrying the thread up and down from the top to the bottom. Maintain the same amount of pulling pressure as you wrap the thread around each notch, and tie the last knot to hold the last warp string as tight as the rest.

The warp should have an even tension across the loom. To tell if your warp has proper tension, place your hand on various parts of the warp. The strings should have enough give for your hand to sink an inch or two before resisting and spring back when you remove your hand. Warp with good tension will act like guitar strings when you strum it. There will be a short vibration and not much give or sag. Uneven tension across the loom will result in difficulty weaving and ripples within your tapestry once it is removed.

LOW-DENSITY VERSUS HIGH-DENSITY WARP

The epi (ends per inch) of your warp determines how thick the yarn that you use as warp is.

The sett of your warp determines how closely your warp strings will be to each other.

A higher sett will allow you to add more detail to your tapestry. It takes longer to weave and has a higher tension, but you can create smoother angles for shapes and curves. To achieve a high-sett warp, loop your warp string around every notch on the loom. Each slit will have two warp strings—one entering and one exiting, and each notch will have one loop around it.

A low sett is perfect for beginners and for quick projects using thicker wefts. Your weave will be looser, have a lower tension, and have a simpler design. To achieve low-sett warp, loop your warp string around every other notch on the loom. Each slip will have one warp string— either exiting or entering—and only every other notch will have a loop around it.

EXTRAS

Mix up your warp to achieve unique effects. Use a contrasting-colored warp string across the entire loom or just one stripe for a pop-up color as it peeks through the weft rows.

You can also mix high- with low-sett warping on the same loom. This is helpful if your project needs detail only in one area of your tapestry and you want the rest to be loose and quick. If you mix warp densities, pay special care to your tension because your weft will be tighter in areas with a higher-warp sett.

Weaving Upside Down

Many weavers work differently, but I recommend the method of weaving upside down. Start from the bottom of your loom and work your way up. With this method the twining header is the first row you complete because it will end up being at the top of the tapestry when it is hung up.

Designing a weave is more flexible if you begin at the tapestry's top instead of with the fringe that hangs off the bottom. You can always add more length to your fringe, it's true, but it is important to have a fixed amount of length reserved for the top loops. You don't want to run out of space by leaving the top for last!

In working from the top of the design to the bottom, there is another problem. Due to a little thing called gravity, your rows will fall down if you push them upward, and it will be harder to maintain consistent tension. When weaving upside down, on the other hand, you beat down the rows. Gravity will be on your side.

This is why I recommend weaving upside down.

Time to Weave

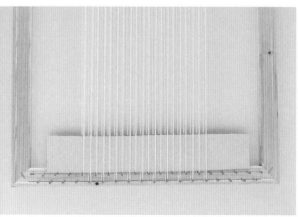

Now that your loom is warped, it's time to begin weaving. However, before you weave your first row, make sure to leave enough warp length at the beginning of the tapestry to knot and tie onto your rod when you are done, about 2". You can use a cardboard guide to help keep the first row straight by cutting a 2" strip of cardboard and weaving it onto the bottom of your loom before adding the twining header rows.

Twining Header

Level: Beginner | Projects: Almost All

The twining header is the first stitch you will complete. It will hold the top of your weave in place once it is completed and removed from the loom. Using a worsted cotton similar or the same as your warp strings will keep the twining header minimal in width, so that it does not distract from the main design. The purpose of the twining header is to evenly space your warp strings, to prepare them for the rows of stitches that will come afterward, and to stabilize the next few rows of stitches to prevent them from sliding down as you weave and once the tapestry is removed from the loom.

1. You will need to begin with a length of string that is about six times the width of your pre-determined tapestry, so measure from the first warp to the last warp six times.

2. Fold this length of string in half to find the center, and then hook the center behind the first warp string on the left so that both of the tails lie in front of the loom.

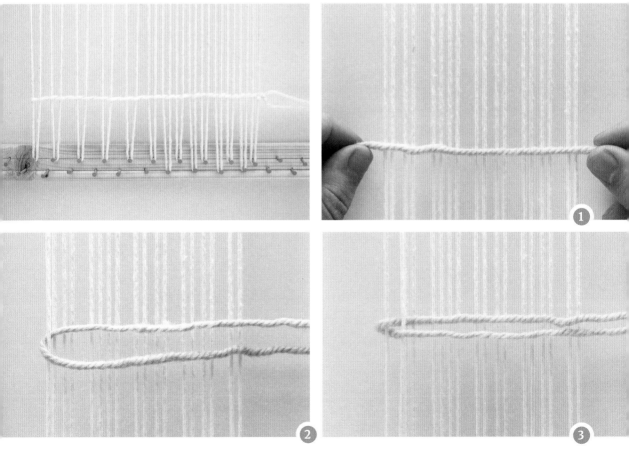

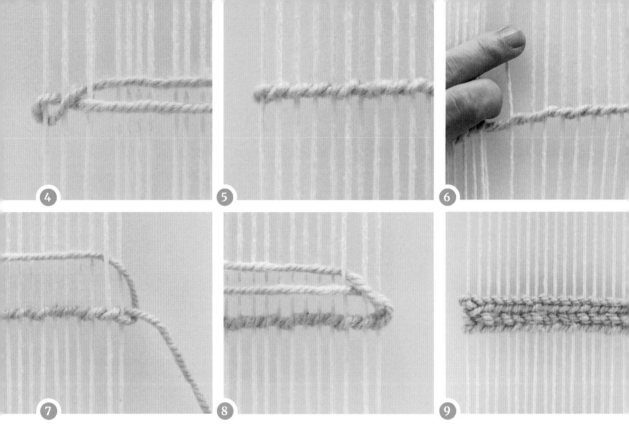

③ When you place the two tails perpendicular to your warp from left to right, you will see that one is on top and the other is on bottom. Begin by slipping the top tail behind the second warp string on the left.

④ Next, take the bottom tail, bringing it over the top tail and slipping it behind the third warp string on the left. Now the top tail is on the bottom and vice versa.

⑤ Repeat these steps until you reach the last warp string on the right. It doesn't matter if your rows of twining arch up. You can beat them into a straight line at the end.

⑥ When you reach the end, hold the top and bottom tails together in one hand and use the other hand to walk across your warp strings, one by one, removing any obvious slack in the twining header. This will make sure the

warp strings are spread evenly and provide extra durability.

⑦ Finish up the full row of twining by turning around and going back to make a second row. To turn around, drop the top tail down, over the bottom tail. Slip the bottom tail behind the second warp string on the right.

⑧ Now you have a top and a bottom again. Continue the same twining stitch by bringing each bottom tail over the top and slipping it behind the next warp string in line until you reach the end of the tapestry again.

⑨ A twining header is usually made of one or two rows, but you are welcome to complete more. Once you have reached the end, tie the two tails together. Use a beater or a comb to push down the two rows of twining until they make a straight line, about 2–3" from the bottom of your warp strings.

Plain Tabby Weave

After the twining header is complete, I always begin with a few rows of plain weave, or tabby, to further stabilize the end of the piece and keep the warp strings evenly spaced for future rows of stitches. The basic tabby is the essential weaving stitch. With the tabby, you can create shapes and cover a lot of space swiftly. It is a flat weave, so the designs created with tabby are two-dimensional, but it is also the foundation for many other tabby stitches that create texture. You can learn more about the different stitches that use tabby as the base at the beginning of the next chapter.

Weft versus Warp Dominant

Tabby works with every type of fiber; however, depending on the thickness of your fiber, there will be differences in the effect. A yarn thinner than your warp will make your rows extra tight and create a "weft dominant" weave, meaning your warp strings will be completely covered up with rows of tabby. If you use yarn thicker than your warp strings, the rows will be looser, and your warp string will be visible as it holds the thick fibers in place. That's a "warp dominant" weave. You can also double up your yarns for a thicker effect, and we'll learn that later in this chapter.

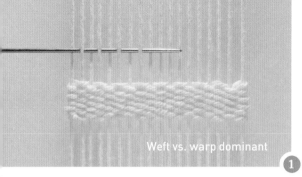

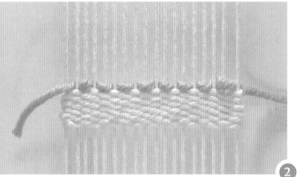

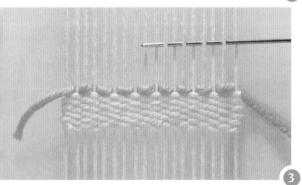

Weft vs. warp dominant

① The plain weave consists of guiding your weft over one warp string and then under the next.

② When you reach the end, you will notice that the weft ends either over or under the last warp string.

③ To turn around, hook the weft in place around the last warp string by beginning over (if you ended under) or under (if you ended over).

That's it! You just learned the most important technique in weaving. You can create almost anything, just by knowing how to plain weave.

Bubbling

Level: Beginner | Projects: Almost All

When your weft is guided straight through as a plain weave, it risks pulling the edges of your tapestry in, especially as you get farther into the middle of the loom, where the warp tension isn't as strong. To stop this from happening, it is essential (VERY IMPORTANT) to relax the tension of your tabby weave with a process called bubbling.

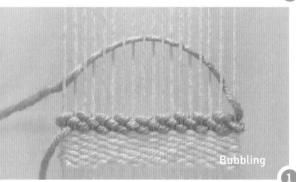

Bubbling

① As you guide your weft through the warp, keep it at least 2–3" above the last row in an arc shape.

② Once you have completed a row, push down weft until it touches the last row every 2–3" to make small hills before beating the row down.

Beating Down Your Rows

Level: Beginner | Projects: Almost All

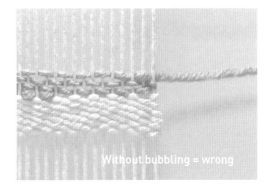

Without bubbling = wrong

Once you have created hills of loose yarn for the bubbling technique, the last step is to beat down your rows. You can use your fingers, a comb, the edge of your shuttle, a beater, or just a regular hairbrush!

Without bubbling and beating, your weft will be pulled too tightly, causing the edges of your weave to be cinched in, and your rows will be too tight to stack properly.

With bubbling and beating, your weft will interlock with the warp in a natural, smooth process as each row is neatly stacked one on top of another.

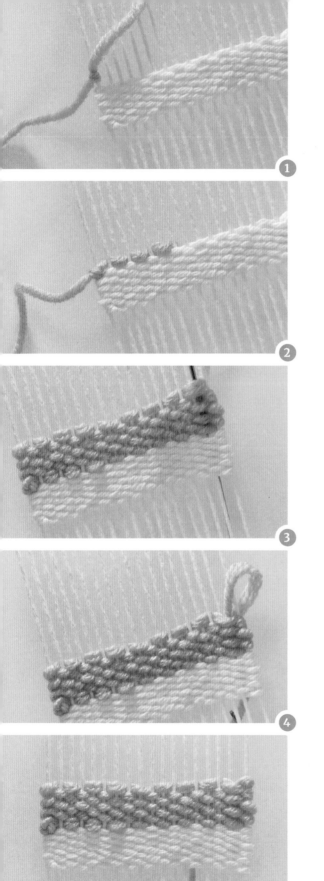

Tucking Tails

When you begin a new fiber, color, or section, you will have to decide how to secure the beginning and end of each row so that they do not come apart when the tension of your warp is released from the loom.

1. When you begin a new row of tabby, leave a tail. You can use a regular overhand knot on the first warp string.

2. The tail should be at least 1" long and will be woven in first or will be left to tuck in at the end. The end of the tail should always exit toward the back of the tapestry.

3. When you reach the end of the last row, thread your needle down through the rows of tabby, parallel to the warp string.

4. Pull your yarn down with the needle. Make sure that the needle exits out the back of the tapestry.

5. As long as you tuck your tail through only the rows that are the same color as the yarn you have just worked with, your ends will be completely hidden and securely attached. The tails on the back of the tapestry will be trimmed later on.

When you get to the end of a section and are ready to move on to a new material, color, or location, you should immediately take care of the leftover tail from your current yarn before continuing. Tucking it in now will save you a lot of time and frustration when you reach the end of your tapestry!

A Word on Clean Weaving

It's easy to get carried away with the design of your tapestry, but neglecting to tuck in the ends immediately after finishing a section will make your job of cleaning up the tapestry much harder at the end.

Weaving the main design of your tapestry is the fun part. Facing a mess to clean up, after you have already worked so hard to make the front of your weave perfect, is very disheartening. You will thank yourself for doing the work in the moment!

The back of a loom will have tucked in tails hanging, ready for an easy trim at the end.

Weaver's Knot

Level: Beginner | Projects: Almost All

A question that new weavers often have is, "How do I know how much yarn to cut for my technique?" If you are using a needle, you will need to pull the yarn through the warp, so you don't want a length that is obnoxiously long. As you continue weaving you will be able to predict how much to cut off more accurately, knowing how much will get used. The important thing to know is that if you do run out of a length of yarn, you can always add more—and that is where the importance of the weaver's knot comes in.

When you reach the end of your yarn but want to continue, either with the same color/material or different, you can use the weaver's knot for a secure, seamless, almost invisible connection.

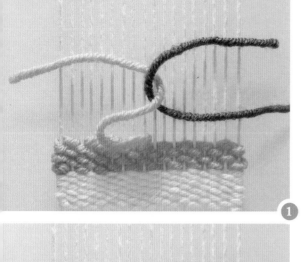

Leave a 2–3" tail from the yarn you are currently working with and cut a new length of yarn. Fold the two tails of both pieces of yarn about an inch in and hook them onto each other.

The end of the new length of yarn is going to wrap around the back of the old length of yarn and down through the center.

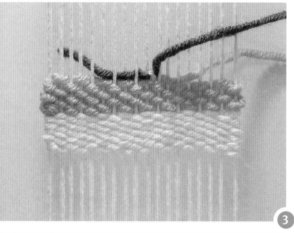

Pull both ends tight to complete the knot. This knot is secure enough that you can cut the two tail ends almost flush to the knot, or you can leave the two tails for added security and tuck them parallel to the row, exiting out the back of the tapestry to be trimmed later on.

To further hide the connection, and minimize the bulge, position the knot head behind a warp string so that it is hidden completely.

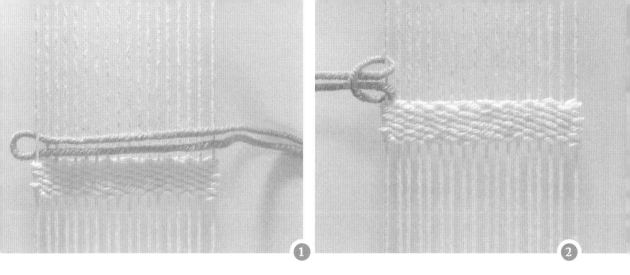

Doubling Up

Level: Beginner | Projects: Any

You can create a thicker weft out of any fiber material by doubling it up for quicker weaving. Use a larkshead knot to secure the end on the warp string you wish to begin on.

① Measure your fiber for the amount you think you might need and then double it. Fold it in half to find the center. Place the fold behind the warp string that you want to start on.

② Pull the two tails through the loop created by the fold so that the knot tightens snugly around the warp string.

③ Weave just like normal with the two tails instead of only one.

④ With two tails the height of your rows is doubled in half the time.

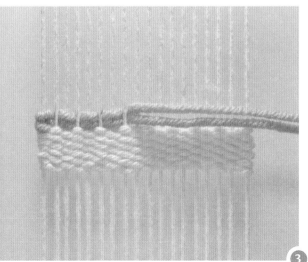

Straight split

Improper tension = gaps

Connecting Edges

When your design includes shapes or colors with rows that lie next to each other, you will frequently run into the decision of how to connect the edges. There are a few different options to choose from.

Straight Split

Level: Beginner | Projects: Geometric Tapestry, p. 122; Full-Fringe Tapestry, p. 125

The first type of edge is called the straight split. It simply means that your vertical edges butt up next to each other but do not cross or connect at all.

1 Weave two separate shapes so that the edges of each one end on parallel warp strings.

2 The edges are very straight and clean.

3 If you attempt to pull the shapes apart, you will notice they are separated, not connected at all.

A straight split is the best way to get a clean, straight edge. However, a straight split can be tricky because it creates a gap in your tapestry. Gaps can be obvious if your edges are pulled in at all due to tension, or if your warp strings are spaced far apart.

A good rule for avoiding gaps in your tapestry is not to straight split more than five vertically stacked rows in a row, depending on the thickness of your yarn.

Joining

Level: Beginner | Projects: Sideways Weave Tapestry, p. 128

Joining is the magical option to keep your straight split on a vertically stacked edge and not have a gap in your tapestry. This is the only way to close a straight split gap and must be done after your edges are woven.

Joining is a technique that sews the edges of your straight split rows together. You want this technique to be a minimal effect, so work from the back of your tapestry and use a thin yarn or thread that won't stand out among the colors of your edges.

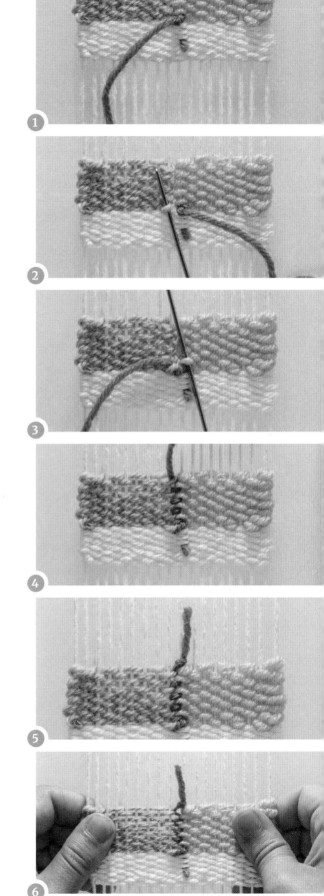

1. Tie a knot onto the first row of your straight split and tuck in the tail.

2. Use your needle to guide the yarn through the loop created by the first row on one side of the straight split.

3. Guide the yarn through the adjacent loop on the other side of the straight split.

4. As you continue working up each row, the gap will be zipped shut by the joining technique. Do not pull the joining too tight or the effect will be more obvious. The goal is simply to hold the gap together so that it appears to be a perfectly straight split that stays closed.

5. Tie a knot at the end of the joining technique, to tuck in later as you continue to add rows above the gap.

6. If you attempt to pull the shapes apart, you will notice that the joining connects them.

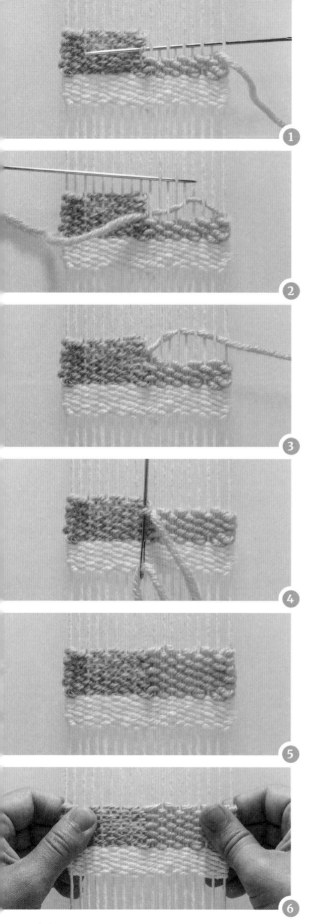

Interlock

Level: Beginner | Projects: Sideways Weave Tapestry, p. 128

Interlocking is another technique to join edges. It is similar to the joining technique but is done as you are weaving, instead of afterward. This is a strong connection that won't gap or be pulled apart; however, it creates a slight ladder effect, so your edges aren't as clean as a straight split.

1 Begin by completing the first shape that will make up one side of the edge. As the rows from your second shape meet the edge, interlock them by guiding your needle through the loop of the adjacent row's edge.

2 When the yarn from the second shape is hooked onto the end of the adjacent row from the first shape, turn around and continuing on to the next row.

3 The two rows are interlocked between warp strings.

4 Continue weaving rows, interlocking each adjacent row.

5 The edges of the two shapes have a slight zipper effect but are still distinct from each other.

6 If you attempt to pull the shapes apart, you will notice that the interlocking connects them.

You can also create a diagonal interlock, which works the exact same, but the rows are stacked as an angle.

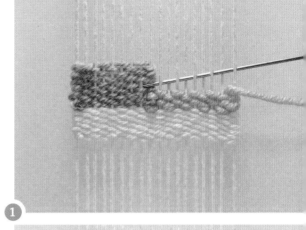

Dovetail

Level: Beginner | Projects: Full-Fringe
Tapestry, p. 125

The dovetail technique is similar to interlocking
but it is quicker than pulling your yarn through
the loops on the edge of each corresponding row.
Dovetail will create a ladder effect and will also
add some bulk to your edge, so it will need to be
beaten down tightly to keep your rows level.

1. Begin as you did with the interlock by
   completing the shape that will make up
   one side of the edge.

2. As the rows from your second shape
   meet the edge, they will pass between
   two of the corresponding rows to loop
   around the warp string of the first edge
   before turning around and continuing
   onto the next row.

3. The edges of the two shapes have a more
   obvious zipper effect.

4. If you attempt to pull the shapes apart,
   you will notice that the dovetailing
   connects them.

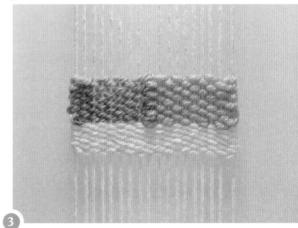

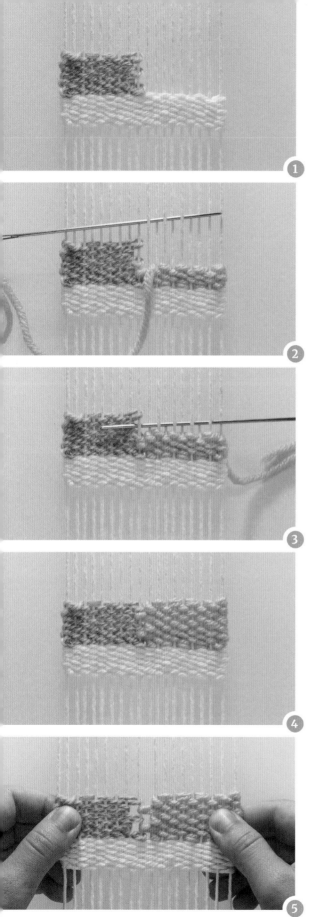

Hatching

Level: Beginner | Projects: Sideways Weave Tapestry, p. 128

Hatching is another technique to join edges. It requires more focus since you are building up the edges of both shapes. It is similar to the dovetail technique but keeps your weft rows even without adding any extra bulk on the edge. It creates the most obvious ladder effect compared to the previous techniques.

1 Complete the first shape. As you are weaving your vertical edge, the ends of each row will alternate between being shorter by one to two warp strings and being longer by one to two warp strings.

2 The adjacent row of the second shape will butt up to the edge without crossing or connecting.

3 Every time one row is short by one warp string, the corresponding row will be long by one warp string to make up for the space.

4 The edges of the two shapes have the most obvious zipper effect.

5 If you attempt to pull the shapes apart, you will notice they separate slightly but the hatching connects them.

You can always combine two of these edge techniques. For example, after completing five rows of straight split, you can connect the edge with one interlocked row before moving on with a few more rows of straight split.

Angles

Connecting angled edges is done similarly to the straight split technique. Adjacent rows butt up to each other on parallel warp strings. However, because of the stairstep technique, there is no splitting and the edges are perfectly connected.

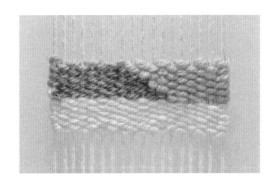

Pick-Up Sticks

Shed Stick

As you are weaving with the tabby stitch, you might start to feel like the process takes a long time to guide your shuttle device over and under each warp string. There are a few ways to speed up the process!

One way is to use a pick-up stick, also known as a shed stick. The "shed" is the space that is created when half of the warp strings are lifted together, allowing your shuttle device to quickly move the weft through, instead of going over and under each warp string individually. You can use many things for your shed stick; a ruler, a strip of cardboard, or an actual shed stick/sword. The stick should be about an inch thick and the width of your tapestry, or the width of the section that you are weaving.

Simply guide the stick over and under your warp strings once, as it is lying flat. When you flip the stick up vertically, it holds the shed between your warp strings open for you to guide your yarn through one row. Then lay it

flat again as you turn around and guide your yarn back through the next row normally, weaving "counter-shed" by manually going over and under each warp string.

As your tapestry gets longer, the tension of your warp strings will get tighter, making it harder to use a shed stick. Eventually you will need to discard the pick-up stick because forcing your warp strings to separate may result in them coming unhooked from your loom.

Removing the Tapestry from the Loom

It's finally time to reveal your tapestry and remove it from the loom. This is my favorite part! Many weavers who leave the job of tucking in their tails until the end dread this last step because it can be a daunting job after they've already been working on a piece for many hours. Did you tuck your ends in as you went? If you did, then the last part is super easy! The key is tucking those ends in as you go, for minimal work at the end.

1. Start by turning your tapestry over and double checking that all of your tails are tucked in, including the first row's twining header.

2. Now all you have to do is trim each tail that is sticking out of the back of your tapestry, knowing that they are secure and won't come undone once the weave is cut off the loom. Your back should be clean and flat.

3. It's time to cut the warp strings. Make sure everything is finished the way you want, because once the warp is cut there is no turning back. You can't fix any mistakes or add anything to your design. Cut only the warp strings that will be at the bottom of your tapestry, leaving the top warp strings as loops.

4. When the warp is cut, pull the loops above the twining header off the loom.

5. The very last element to secure your weave is to add a regular overhand knot on each of the top loops, right above the twining header.

Once your warp is cut, your tapestry will be at its most vulnerable, which is why it is so important to have a twining header at the top and a hem stitch at the bottom, with your design sandwiched in between. The twining

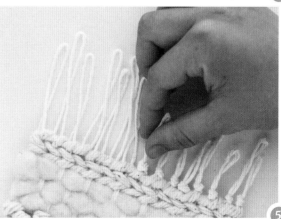

header is essential for your weave at this point because it holds all of your rows in place from the top. It is so satisfying seeing all the little extra steps pay off in the end.

If you finished with fringe rya, you can leave the bottom warp strings because they will be covered by a wall of fringe. However, if you want a straight border on the bottom of your tapestry, you can tuck each warp string up through the back of your tapestry, just as you do when tucking in ends.

Your loom has finished its job with this project, so you can set it aside until you're ready to warp it up for your next tapestry.

Attaching the Rod

There are a few ways to hang your weave. You can read about different types of rods on page 25. There are also other ways to display your weaving projects, which can be found later in the book.

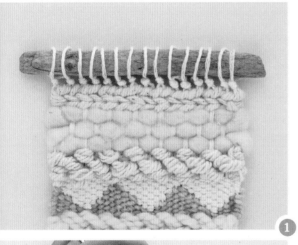

Knot and Slip

The first way to attach your tapestry to a rod is the simplest. After you have completed the overhand knots on each loop at the top of your tapestry, simply slide your rod through. This works best with a rod that is completely straight and smooth, with nothing for the loops to catch on. It also works best if your loops are smaller, just barely wider than the width of your rod so that there isn't excess space to let the tapestry slide off.

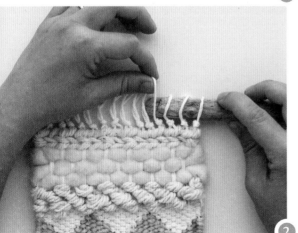

1 Start from the end, with the first loop, and gently guide the rod through by holding the loop open with your fingers. Then move onto the next loop, and slide the rod farther.

2 Complete this all the way to the end, and then go back and space the loops out evenly. Cut a piece of string just longer than the rod and tie it on the rod on either side of the tapestry.

Sewing On

This is my personal technique to attach a weave to a stick. It is very forgiving and results in a mildly adjustable hold. It works with any tapestry that has loops at the top, and the loops don't even have to be the same length, so this is the perfect option to use with the loom that you made at the beginning of the book. The best part is that your stick doesn't have to be smooth, thin, or consistent enough to slip your loops around! I tell all my students that this is my GAMECHANGER technique, and once they try it out they always come back to agree.

Begin by adding a regular overhand knot with each loop pair above your twining header, just as you would with the slip method.

Once all of your loops are knotted, turn your weave so that you are facing the backside and lay it down on a table. Cut a long length of string that is the same material as your warp.

(Step-by-step pictures on following page)

1 Starting from the right, tuck the tail and use a single knot to secure the length of yarn onto the first warp string, below the overhand knot. Position your stick in place.

2 Thread your yarn through the front of the first loop on the other side of the stick.

3 Pull it tight toward the back again. It will wrap around your stick.

4 Now thread your string through the back of the next loop, between the two warp strings below the overhand knot. Then thread it through the front of the second loop on the other side of the stick.

5 Continue threading the yarn through the front of each loop and below each overhand knot, moving across the top of the tapestry.

6 Once you reach the end, tie as knot on the last warp string and tuck the tail. Create a hanger by tying a length of yarn on either side of your stick so that you can hang it up.

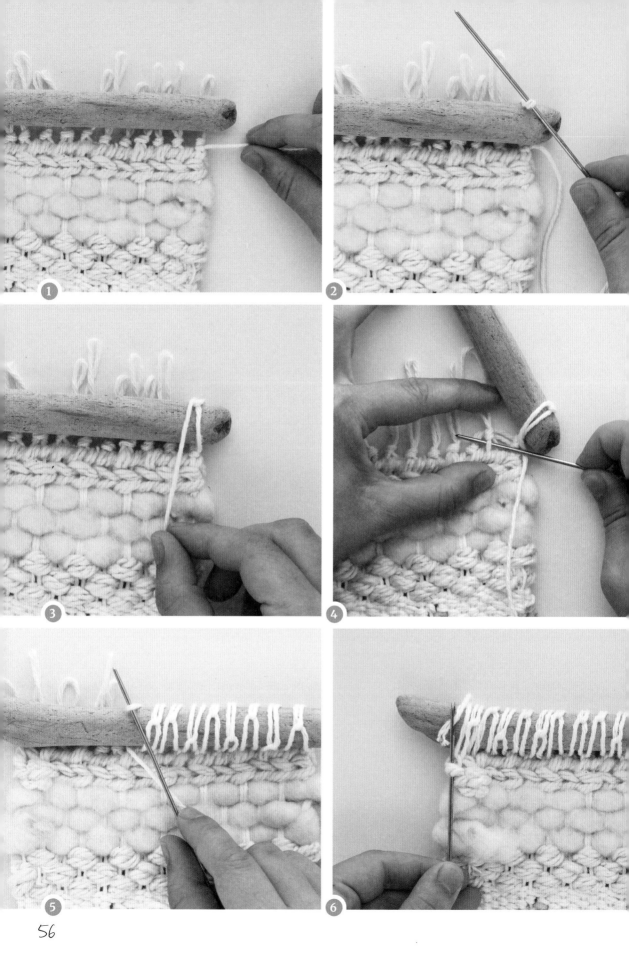

Tuck and Wrap

This technique is a bit more polished and stylized. It is also very forgiving and great for attaching curved sticks because the top of the tapestry is connected to the rod only in places you choose. This technique requires good judgment so that the piece is secured to the rod often enough and with enough wrapping so that the weight of the tapestry is supported.

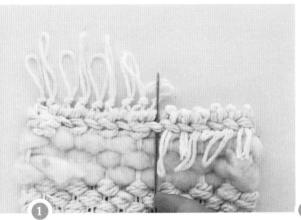

Begin by tucking in each loop at the top of your tapestry through the first row or two on the back of your tapestry. This will create a clean edge on top.

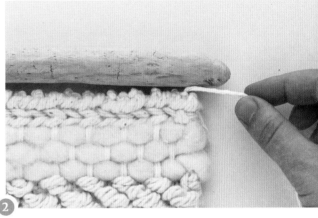

Tie a length of yarn onto a top warp string in the area you wish to attach the rod.

Wrap the yarn around the rod and through the first row or overhand knots of the tapestry. Wrap as much or as little as you want and then tie a knot and tuck the tail.

Create a hanger by tying a length of yarn on either side of your stick so that you can hang it up.

Problem Solving

There's nothing more frustrating than taking your tapestry off the loom and seeing it pucker or bulge in places that appeared completely straight when your warp strings were taut. It will help to keep in mind as you weave that usually any problems you have while on the loom will be magnified when you cut your tapestry off the loom. As you gain more skill as a weaver, you will understand how to avoid these mistakes by using different materials and techniques.

Post-Straightening

If you find yourself in panic mode with a tapestry that has already been cut off the loom and is bulging or puckering, you can try a technique called blocking. Lay your weave on a towel and, with an iron, apply steam as you flatten or straighten any problem spots. Place another towel on top with some books or a weight to hold it in place as it dries.

This method may work if you happened to use natural materials that have enough flexibility to stretch from the steam. However, this solution introduces problems of its own. It won't fix any tension issues completely, it will flatten your texture, and the steam will make your fibers expand to be more vulnerable to pilling and getting dusty. In the end you may have to accept the changes as adding "character" to your tapestry, and move forward with a lesson learned.

The best way to assure that your tapestry will look the same off the loom as it did on the loom is by avoiding any problems AS you are weaving. Here are some of the most common problems and how to avoid them:

GAPS

This happens when you have two parallel straight split borders that are more than 1" tall running vertically along your warp strings. If you don't use any type of connecting technique, such as hatching or interlocking, these edges will separate when your warp strings are cut off. If you don't mind the separation, don't worry, but if your rows are pulled too tightly, the separations will turn into curved gaps . . . which look much worse than just simple slits.

To avoid this problem, it is better to err on the side of weaving your rows a bit too loose, to cover up any gap. Better yet, use a hatching or interlocking technique to make sure they are closed. Learn more about connecting edges on page 46.

SHRINKAGE

Did you know that all tapestries shrink a bit when they are taken off the loom? Both the length and width of a weave will shrink when the tension is released. This is completely normal, but the amount depends on the materials you use. If exact size is extra important to you, add two to four extra warp strings to your piece's normal number to compensate for any loss in size.

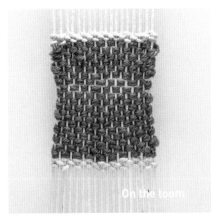
On the loom

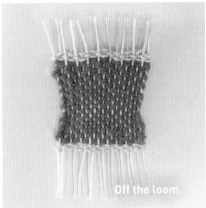
Off the loom

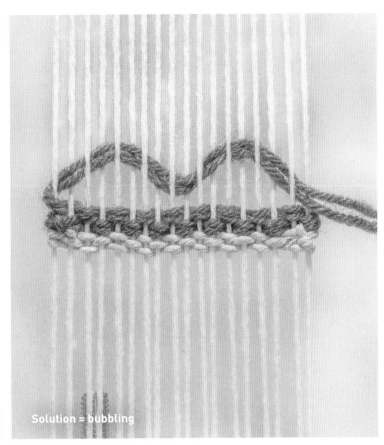
Solution = bubbling

CONCAVE EDGES

This is the most common problem that weavers face—especially beginning weavers—so don't be discouraged if your first few tapestries curve in a bit on the sides. This happens when the tension on your rows is too tight. It becomes most obvious as you reach the middle of your tapestry's length, because the farther your selvedge is from the support of the loom notches, the less tension it has to hold your sides straight.

The most important thing you can do to avoid this problem is: Don't forget the bubbling technique! The mounds that you create from your rows before you beat them down are critical when it comes to keeping the tension of your tapestry even.

If you complete a section and notice that your selvedges are curving in, I don't recommend going back and releasing the tension by simply letting yarn out on each row. You won't be able to bubble the weft, which means that chances are it will mess up your tension even more by pulling in the warp strings in different places within the tapestry. The best, highest-quality way to successfully fix a curved selvedge is to watch out for it carefully and undo the problem rows before moving on.

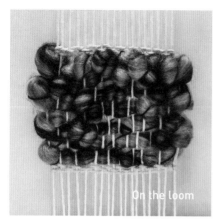

On the loom

Off the loom

Solution = twining

CONVEX EDGES

This is the opposite problem of selvedges that cave inward, and usually happens because you use a thicker material, such as roving, even if it is surrounded by regular-size yarn. Convex edges happen for the same reason concave edges do—the tension of your warp strings is weaker in the middle the farther it gets from the support of your frame loom. If you are using thick yarn, it will spread out the warp strings and will cause the tapestry edges to curve outward.

The best way to fix this problem is to add a "tension check" row or two of twining within the section of thick yarn to hold the warp strings evenly in place. You can even use a very thin thread for the twining row. The twining will likely be covered by the thick yarn, so it will be hidden and won't affect your overall design.

SURFACE BULGING

This problem isn't obvious until you cut your tapestry off the loom and the tension is released. When surface bulging happens, the surface of your tapestry does not lie flat. It is warped into waves of hills and valleys.

When the tension is released, the tapestry rebounds because the warp is no longer being pulled straight. If there are spots that are woven tighter than others, they will pull the weakened warp in, and if there are spots that are woven loosely, they will expand the warp out. The competing tension of the two will cause the warp to pucker into a bowl shape or bulge into a bump. As you experiment with combining multiple materials with different thicknesses and elasticity, you will become more skilled at making up for the tension differences so that the tension stays even across all sections.

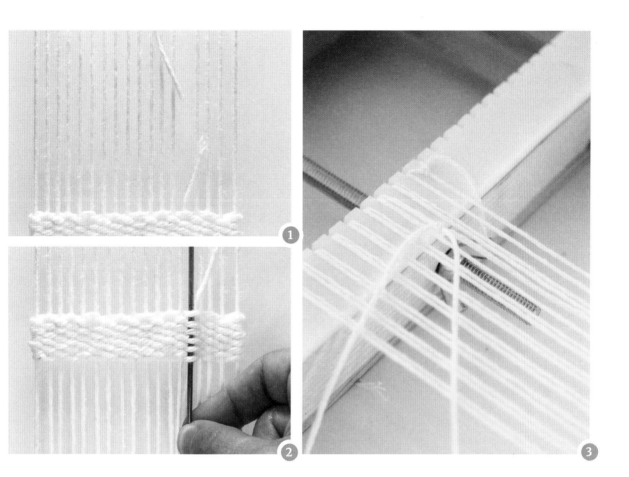

Materials that are stretchy are difficult to weave with and cause bulging problems. To be safe when using elastic materials, weave extra loosely with them so that you aren't accidentally pulling them too tightly.

Another possible cause could be due to your execution of shapes. Tabby should always run perpendicular to your warp. Instead of angling your rows to match the angle of your shape, create many horizontal rows with edges that are stacked to create the boundaries of your shape. Creating tabby rows on an angle or a curve will make your weave pucker and bulge when it is taken off the loom.

BROKEN WARP STRING

What if your scissors slip and you accidentally cut a warp string in the middle of a design!?

This happens to everyone. Do not panic: there are ways to fix it.

1 Assess the location of your breakage. If the tail is long enough to tie in a short length of warp yarn to connect the break, then that is the easiest fix. If the tail is cut too close to your design for this, you may need to pull it out and replace the single length of warp string.

2 Before you pull out the warp string, use it as a guide to tuck your needle through the affected weft rows and pull through a replacement warp string. Then remove the broken warp.

3 Tie the replacement warp onto the existing warp with a weaving knot. It is best to connect them at the top of your loom, so that the knot won't interfere as you continue to weave.

Preserving Tapestries

You may wonder what the best practices are to preserve your tapestry once it is completed. After all of your hard work, how do you keep it looking new so that it can hang in your home as long as possible? Here are a few ways to be sure your tapestry will continue to look as good as the day you cut it off the loom.

Frame it. The best way is to frame your tapestry. Just like regular artwork, putting your art behind glass is the best way to be sure it stays safe and clean. However, some tapestries are much too big to fit in a frame, and the detail of the texture can't be appreciated when there are "walls" around it.

Hang it high. Hang your tapestry on a wall high enough that children's interested little hands can't tug on the fringe or pull it off.

Don't touch it. If you do have to take it down or move it, don't leave it sitting around or wadded up. Try to find a different place to hang it temporarily. The less your tapestry is touched or comes in contact with other objects, the longer it will last.

Don't use roving. It is sad, but some materials are better than others when it comes to longevity. Roving is more prone to dust, grime, and snags. It is also known to attract bugs if you live in a humid area, because the fluffy fibers are not spun tightly together. If you truly love roving in your work, try to frame it or accept that you should enjoy your piece while it lasts.

Don't hang it in a kitchen. Grease, grime, steam, and strong smells all are enemies of woven tapestries. That's why your kitchen is not the ideal place to hang your tapestry. Instead, hang it in a well-ventilated, dry location.

Hang it away from the sun. Some dyes can fade in sunlight over time. If you want your colors to stay vibrant, keep the tapestry away from a sunny spot.

Minimal cleaning. If you find that your tapestry is getting dusty and you want to be proactive, you can lightly clean it. The best way to clean fibers is regular dusting with a lint roller or with an upholstery attachment on your vacuum. Place a synthetic mesh such as hosiery over the top. If your piece has small beads, make sure they cannot be pulled through the mesh or dislodged from the tapestry.

Framing a Tapestry

Level: Beginner | Projects: Any

One of my favorite ways to display a tapestry is by framing it. Not only does this protect the tapestry, but it makes it stand out among pieces on a gallery wall and is a great way to gift a tapestry to someone. When framed, it can make your work look more professional and will preserve it for many more years than if it was just hanging directly on the wall.

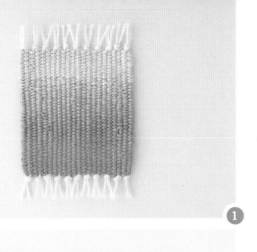

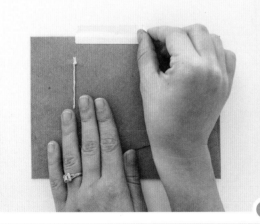

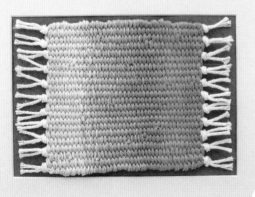

You can take your tapestry to a local framing store for help in mounting it into a frame, or you can easily do it yourself at home.

1. The first step is to find a frame that will fit your tapestry, or create a tapestry to fit your frame. Many people use shadowboxes with enough depth. This will help if your tapestry has a lot of texture that you don't want pressed up against the glass. However, if you can't find a shadowbox that will fit your tapestry, you can simply remove the glass and use the frame without it. This technique will not protect the tapestry, but it will give it a frame for display purposes.

2. Once you have a frame that is the appropriate size, the next step is to sew your tapestry onto a backing that can be held within the frame. Find a stiff card stock in the color of your choice and cut the stock so that it fits the frame. Center your tapestry on the backing of your choice and use a piece or two of double-sided tape to hold it in place. Use a sharp needle and some yarn in the same color as your outer weave to sew the edges of your tapestry to the backing so that it is sturdy. The stitches should be invisible so that the tapestry appears to be hanging on the backing with no support.

3. If you choose to include extra space between your tapestry and the edge, you can factor in the size of a mat to border your tapestry before the frame begins.

4. Now that your tapestry is sewn onto the backing, simply place the backing with the mat into your picture frame and close the back of your frame.

Section 3
FOUNDATIONAL TECHNIQUES

Tabby/Plain Weave

We covered the basics of the plain tabby weave, but there are even more ways you can use it! Tabby is the most versatile technique, one that will allow you to create almost any design you can think of.

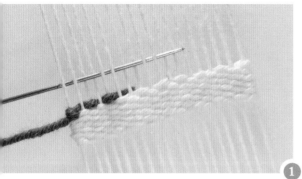

Floating Tabby

Level: Beginner | Projects: Practice, p. 116

You can speed up the tabby technique by floating, which means going over and under two or more warp strings at a time. Tabby is always a balanced weave, so however many warp strings you go over, you will go under the same amount.

1. Tie a knot and weave in the tail.

2. Go over and under two warp strings at a time instead of one.

3. This is also a good way to use thicker yarns, or more than one yarn at a time.

4. Floating tabby allows you to cover a large space quickly.

Unbalanced floating tabby is also known as twill. We explore it in my book *Welcome to Weaving 2*.

Hooking

The key to getting vertical lines is to go over the same warp strings with only the same color. So, when you begin each row, pay attention to how the color ended on the last row you used it on. Start by going over or under the last warp string, depending on if the same color ended by going over or under the last warp string.

If your yarn ended under the last warp string, it will need to go over the second yarn before turning around and going under the same warp string for the next row. This will hook it in place on the end.

Pick and Pick

Level: Beginner | Projects: Geometric, p. 122

Ready to learn some more ways to use the basic tabby weave? Let's make some vertical stripes! You will need two different colors for this technique, and they need to be about the same thickness as each other.

1. Start by completing one row of tabby with the first color.

2. Next, take the second color and create the next row of tabby, starting from the same side, but going under and over the opposite warp strings as you did on the first row of color.

3. To start the third row, go back to using your first color. If your yarn ended under the last warp string, it will need to go over the second yarn before turning around and going under the

same warp string for the next row. This will hook it in place on the end.

4. Use the second yarn to go over and under the same warp strings that it did before.

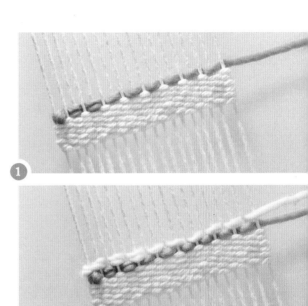

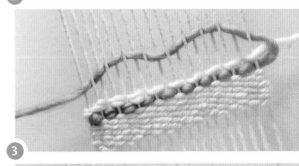

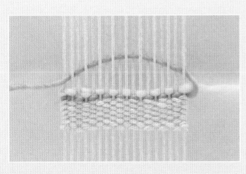

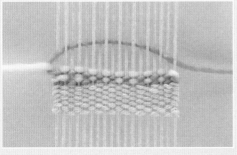

5

Finish by threading the tail of each color down through their own colored stripes to help hide the ends, just as you did with the tabby weave.

6

The illusion behind this method works because you alternate colors with each row, so that stripes appear to climb vertically as you move the tabby stitch over and under the warp strings. The tighter you pack these rows, the more obvious the pattern will be.

Stripes

Level: Beginner | Projects: Basic Sampler, p. 119; Geometric Tapestry, p. 122

Horizontal stripes are a simple method using the basic tabby method. By alternating every few rows of tabby with different colors, you can create stripes that run horizontally on your tapestry.

Create thinner stripes by completing fewer rows before changing colors, or thicker stripes by completing more rows before changing colors. You can also create free-form stripes by mixing thick and thin stripes, using more or fewer rows for different colors.

If your rows are thinner, you don't have to tuck your ends and cut at the end of each color section. Simply leave the tail of one color free as you add a row of different colors, and then go back to using the tail of the color as you begin your next row.

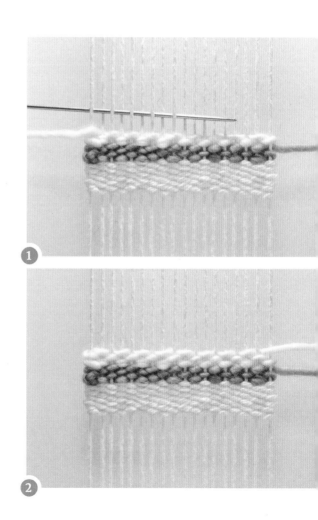

1

2

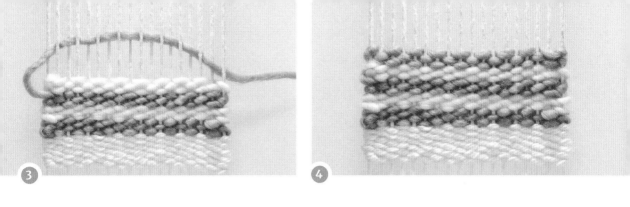

Weaving with Chunky Yarn

Level: Beginner | Projects: Any

Weaving with chunkier yarns can result in fun, bold effects, but sometimes they prove a bit of a challenge compared to other yarns. Don't let this hold you back! Thick yarns are classified as yarns that are about the width of your pinky finger. They are often spun around a core, which means they are stiffer. Unlike regular yarns, it's more difficult to tuck the tails of thick yarn, and knots are much more visible. One of the best things to do when working with chunky yarn is to embrace the added lumps and bumps as part of the style that chunky yarns often bring to weaving. Any problems you run into while weaving with chunky yarns can be fixed if you keep these pointers in mind.

Tucking Chunky Tails

The first challenge to working with chunky yarns is how to begin and end. In the example shown in the first photo, their bulk will be helpful because the extra tension helps to hold them in place better than a regular-thickness yarn. This technique will leave you with clean, secure ends that are practically invisible.

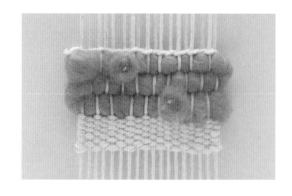

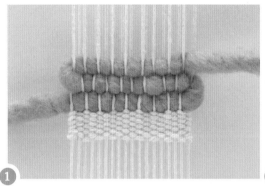

1 Leave a 2–3" tail out of the back of the tapestry at the beginning and end of the chunky yarns, without knotting or tucking.

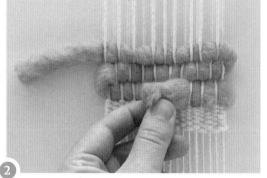

2 When you finish the section, turn your loom around and weave the tails in parallel to the rows of thick yarn, under and over the same warp strings.

Twining Row to Organize Warps

The most common problem is that thick yarn can make your warp strings line up unevenly. Even when you try your best to keep them spaced properly, thick material can take them off course as the shed is spread apart. An easy fix for warp strings that have become uneven is to follow up a section of chunky yarn with a row or two of twining. This technique is the best method to get your warp strings back in place so that you can continue an even weave with good tension.

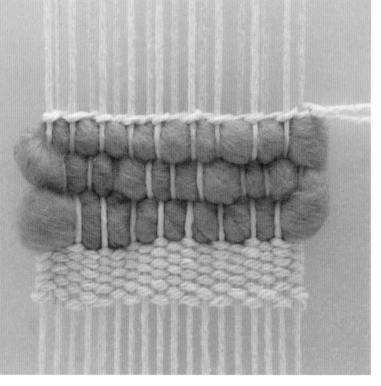

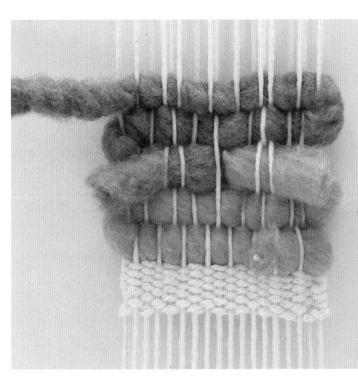

Adding Lengths

The last tip to keep in mind is that weaver's knots rarely work with thick yarn. If you run out of a length of yarn but want to continue the same material in the section, you will need to finish the two tails by tucking them behind the tapestry. There will be a gap where the two ends meet, but it will be less noticeable than the giant bulge that a weaver's knot would create with thick yarn.

With these tips you should be able to weave confidently with chunky yarn. However, there are some techniques that just won't work with thick yarn the way they would with regular yarn. For example, weaving shapes is difficult because your edges won't be very smooth. The two best techniques to use with thick yarn are tabby and soumak.

Weaving with Roving

Roving is a beautiful material that will add a distinct style to your tapestry. Many of the techniques and challenges that you run into with chunky yarn will also apply to roving, but roving is much more flexible to mold and twist.

Ripping Roving

Roving is a stage of fiber before it has been twisted into the traditional shape of a yarn strand. Although the fibers have been cleaned and combed so that they line up, they are fragile at this point and can easily rip when they are pulled with too much pressure.

Rip . . .

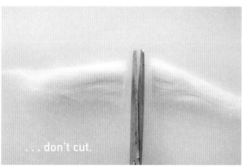

. . . don't cut.

While this is a potential problem while weaving, it is also important to know for separating your roving into sections. Unlike yarn, you should never use scissors to cut roving. The fibers must be ripped for the material to work naturally.

Tucking Roving Tails

Managing the tails of roving stitches requires a different approach than regular yarn because it is too thick to use a needle to tuck the tails

down among the warp strings. Instead, use the same technique that you would with chunky yarn to weave the ends in among the previous row of weft.

Roving is very flexible, so it is best to use your hands instead of a needle or shuttle when adding it to your tapestry. Molding it to be thick or thin, tight or loose, and deciding whether to twist it are all part of your personal technique when it comes to roving.

Twisting

Because roving is not twisted, it helps improve the durability of your tapestry to twist it yourself as you weave. If you want to maximize the texture from your roving, twist it through a regular tabby row and then pull it out in loops so that the material appears to be bubbling on the surface. Twist it while creating soumak as well to give the technique your preferred shape.

Roving adds loose, thick texture to tapestries, but keep in mind that it lacks durability. Roving can attract dust and grime more easily than spun yarn because the fibers are not twisted closed. It can also snag more easily and is harder to clean, so roving is not the best material to use if you want your tapestry to last a long time.

The best techniques to use with roving are tabby and soumak, but many weavers also use it for rya fringe. Again, this is a style that I don't recommend because the fibers can't be combed and are more prone to coming loose, which limits the longevity of the hard work you put into your tapestry.

Free-Form Loops with Roving

Level: Beginner | Projects: Any

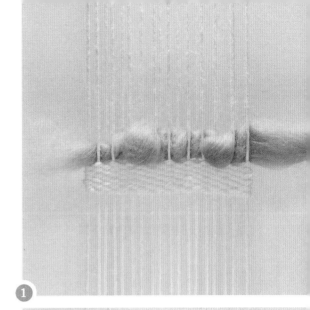

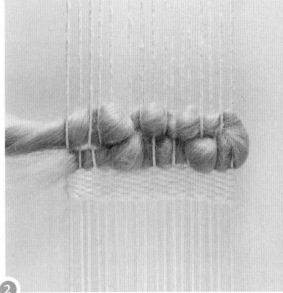

If you want to create a loop effect where each loop is a different size, simply pull out yarn from between the warp strings of your row with your fingers.

1. Complete a row of tabby, twisting as you weave. Use your fingers to pull out a few bumps of roving between the warps.

2. You will need to begin your loops from the side that is continuing from the last row and work your way to the side that has the excess tail. This ensures that you will be pulling the extra yarn for your loops from the tail and will maintain your tension.

3. The thickness of the material and loops may make the sides of your tapestry bow out in a convex arc and upset the organization of your warp strings, so add an invisible twining row among the loops and above the technique to keep your sides straight. Read more about this in the problem-solving section of the book on page 58.

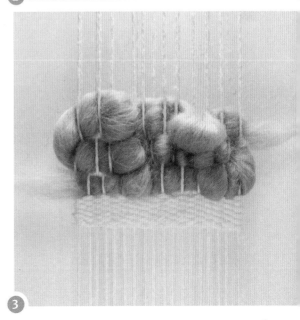

Soumak Roving Braid

Level: Beginner | Projects: Any

Soumak is a technique that creates wraps around warp strings to create an overlapping braided effect. Roving is perfect for creating beautiful braids of soumak. You can alter the effect of this technique by using thick or thinner pieces of roving and tight or loose soumak.

1. Leave a tail and wrap your roving around every three to four warp strings, twisting as you go to keep the braid smooth.

2. When you reach the end, complete a second row to create a full braid effect.

3. You can either use a needle to pull the thinned-out ends through the back of the fibers for a flat edge or tuck them in like chunky yarn, or tie a knot in the back and weave in the remaining tail.

4. As with other techniques for thick yarn, pay attention to the bulk that roving adds to your tapestry, in case you need to reorganize your warps to keep your sides straight.

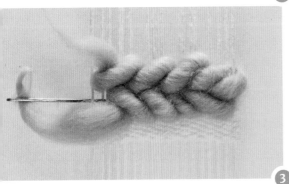

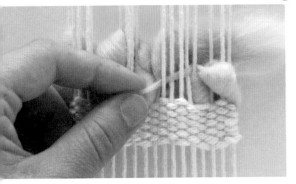

Shapes

Weaving shapes is essential for almost any design you will come up with. Some may be obvious while others seem daunting (circles!), but when you know the basics of how to weave shapes, the possibilities are endless.

Shapes are simply rows of regular weaving techniques. Paying attention to where the edges of these regular rows begin and end is the key to creating shapes. To create different angles for your shapes, you must pay attention to the ratio of your warp to weft.

Planning Angles

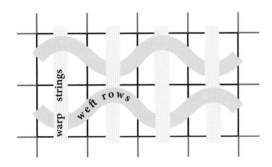

Straight lines	45-degree angle
0 : 1+ or 1+ : 0	1 : 1

Sharp horizontal	Sharp vertical
1 : 2+	2+ : 1

Deciding which ratio to use for different parts of your shape depends on three things.

1. The size of your shape (giant circles will need a larger ratio than small circles).

2. The width of your yarn (thin yarn will need to build up more rows than thick yarn). The best yarn to use for easy ratios is the same thickness as the space between your warp strings.

3. The angle of the edge you are working on. Acute versus obtuse versus straight all will need different ratios. See the examples on the next page.

Planning Shapes

You can always weave with no plan, but if the size and placement of your shape is important to the design, there are a few ways to plan your shape. You can draw or print out a template to pin behind your warp and follow that, or you can draw straight on to your warp (the photos in the instructions show you both ways).

When you have a design to follow, it is best to weave from the bottom and build up, but if your design has elements that you want in a specific location, you can begin by weaving these "floating shapes" and fill in around them.

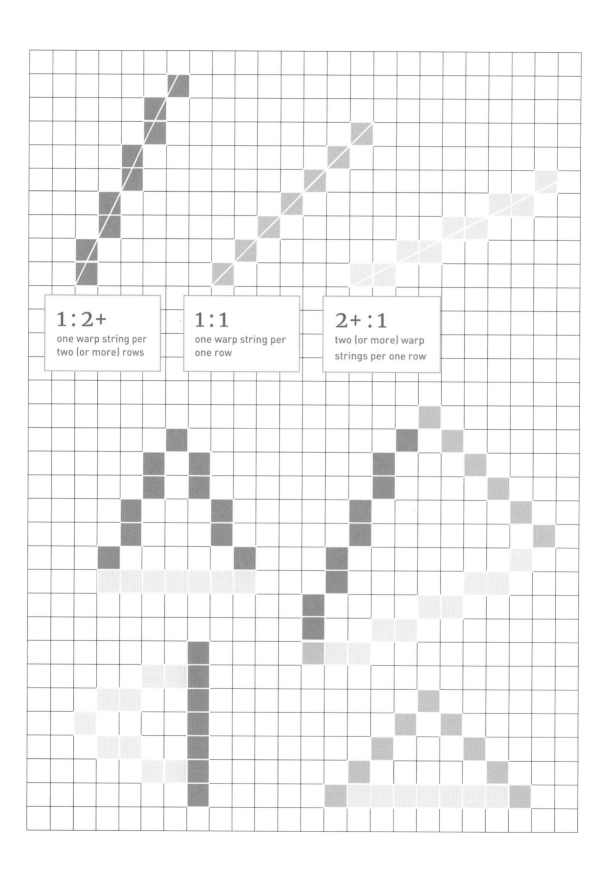

1 : 2+
one warp string per two (or more) rows

1 : 1
one warp string per one row

2+ : 1
two (or more) warp strings per one row

Circles

Circles can be daunting, but the result is impressive in a tapestry. The math involved to create a circle is based on the size, thickness of material, and warp sett. Remember that the sides of shapes are simply stairsteps created at different angles. Circles are created by angles that are straight across to begin, then slightly horizontal, then 45 degrees, then slightly vertical, and then straight up and down before reflecting the previous angles in reverse order. If you keep these angles in mind, it is easier to create a perfect circle freehand.

TEMPLATES

Although it is possible to create perfect circles freehand, many skilled weavers use a template to make the job easier.

1. Use a cup or circular object to trace a circular shape on your warp with a light-colored felt-tip marker.

2. The shape of the circle will be outlined for you to fill in.

3. Begin by filling in the outside of the circle, halfway up the sides.

4. Fill in the entire circle. Remember that the top should reflect the bottom, so pay attention to your rows from the bottom half as you weave.

5. Fill in the outside of the circle from the halfway point.

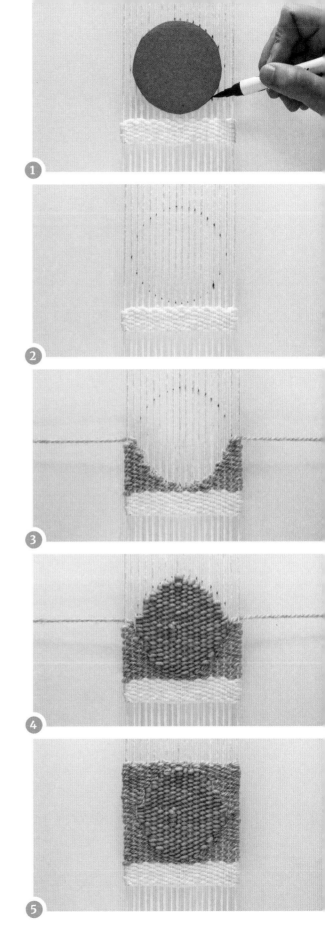

Blocks

Level: Beginner | Projects: Geometric
Tapestry, p. 122

The easiest shape is a simple block. The bottom
is a straight row, the sides are straight vertical
rows, which all begin and end on the same
warp strings, and the top is a straight row as
well. When you create blocks, make sure you
pay attention to your vertical sides to decide
how/if you should connect them to any
neighboring edges to avoid gaps in your
tapestry. (See more on page 46.)

Triangles

Level: Beginner | Projects: Basic Sampler,
p. 119; Geometric, p. 122; Circular Star, p. 131

Besides blocks, triangles are the simplest
shape you can make. They are good practice for
weaving angles, especially when your triangle
is not symmetrical.

The edges of triangles and shapes are like
stairsteps. The number of rows you stack up
versus the number of warp strings you pass
over create your edges. To create a triangle,
simply go over fewer and fewer warp strings as
you build up your rows. Center the number of
warp strings to keep the triangle symmetrical,
or work on the angle of each side differently for
a triangle that is not equilateral.

For a steeper edge, stack more rows before
removing a warp string, and for shallower
rows, remove more than one warp string at a
time for each row.

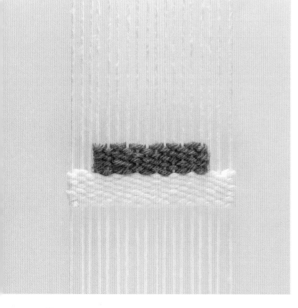

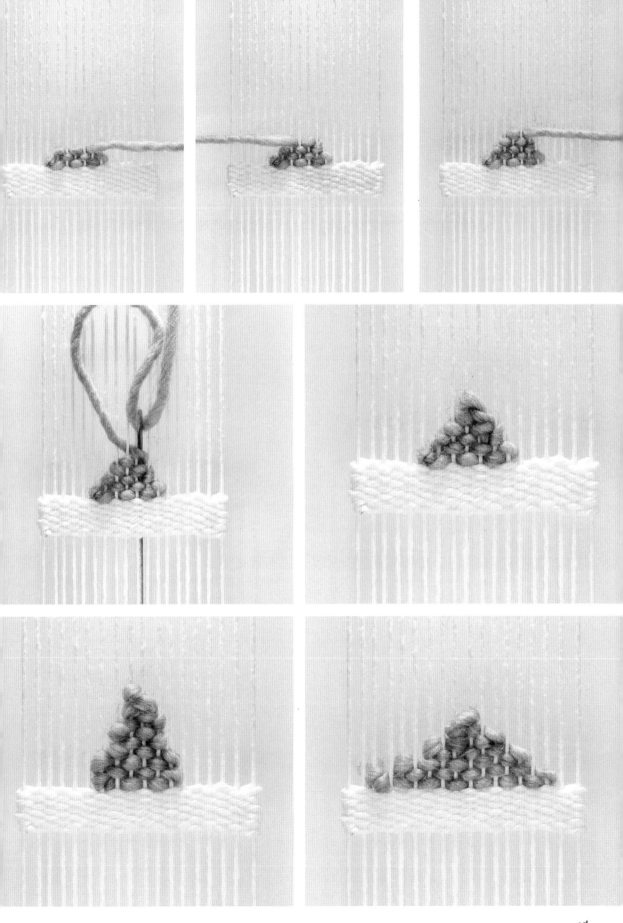

Pictures

What about shapes that are not symmetrical or blocky, or that resemble an object? The best way to approach these types of shapes is to imagine them broken up into smaller, more-manageable shapes. If your object needs to stay true to a picture, use a template. You can either trace the template onto your warp or keep the picture clipped to your warp for reference.

1. Begin at the bottom and work your way up so that as you are building the picture's shape, it is supported by previous rows.

2. If there are separate pieces that protrude out of the sides of the shape, take turns weaving each side from the bottom up.

3. Use the hatching or interlock technique to combine each section with the bigger picture.

4. You can weave multiple separate shapes throughout your tapestry and then go back and fill in the background, or complete the background as you are weaving the picture shape.

Tapestry weavers who create detailed imagery begin from the bottom of the loom and build the picture up, working on the background and the shape together so that whatever section they are working on never gets boxed in. This ensures an even tension across the surface of the tapestry.

Free-Form

Level: Beginner | Projects: Sideways Weave
Tapestry, p. 128

Free-form is a technique that you can use when you don't have, or don't want, a plan of how your tapestry will look by the end. That's why it is called free-form, because you are free to improvise.

1. When you weave in free-form, you do not limit yourself to weaving rows horizontally. You may build up one section at a time and then guide your weft as a single row to a different spot on the loom to continue with a new section.

2. You may weave your rows as curves or diagonals to crawl up the side of a shape. You may also switch up your materials on a whim or throw in a bit of twill or a random rya knot.

3. Free-form works well with twining and soumak techniques as well because they allow your curves and shapes to be more fluid.

4. The important thing to remember when you weave free-form is to pay attention that any strong vertical edges are properly connected so that there is no gapping. You should also make sure to weave loosely, especially if you are weaving curves, so that your tension does not draw in the sides.

Free-form weaving is a great way to use your skills in a therapeutic way. Without paying attention to the rules, you are allowing the fibers to show you how they can best be used.

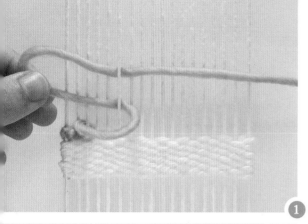

Soumak

Level: Beginner | Projects: Basic Sampler, p. 119; Circular Star Weave, p. 131

The soumak technique is one of the most versatile methods, besides twining and tabby. Soumak looks similar to the twining stitch, but you work with only one tail, looping the weft around the warp strings. This technique looks great with a thick, loosely spun fiber such as roving because it resembles large braids across your tapestry. It is one of the best techniques to create organic movement because it works well in curved shapes. There are also many ways to add subtle differences that will transform the soumak to look like a completely new technique.

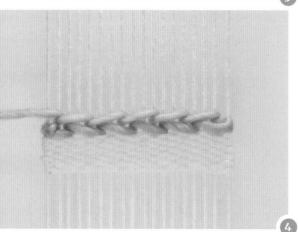

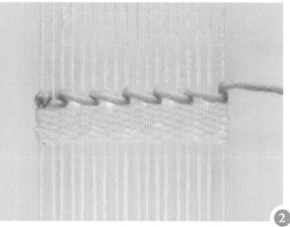

1 Begin the soumak the same way you would with a tabby weave, by tying the end. The basic soumak wraps the yarn in front of two to four warp strings and then backward behind one warp string before pulling the tail up through the center of the two warp strings and repeating.

2 The technique creates a stacked domino effect.

3 When you turn around to create a second row, wrap the yarn around one warp string to the right of the row below to spread out the bulk of the wraps.

4 Complete two rows of soumak, going opposite ways for the overlapping effect to resemble a herringbone braid pattern.

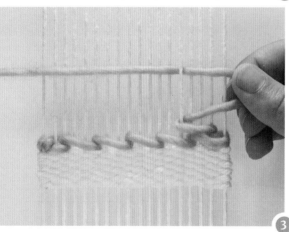

Soumak can also be used in a varied pattern by going over three, back behind two, over four, back behind one, etc. It can also be reversed so that the weft goes behind two warp strings first and then backward toward the front around one warp string, etc.

When you reach the end of your row, you can tuck the tails of normal yarn up through the rows, just like tabby. If you are using roving, refer to the chapter about roving to learn how to manage your ends.

Experiment with soumak by using multiple rows of smaller yarn or giant twists of thick roving.

Egyptian Knot

Level: Beginner | Projects: Any

By simply reversing the soumak technique, you will create a completely different effect called the Egyptian Knot. You can space the knots out or keep them close together in a line.

Instead of wrapping the yarn in front your warp strings, wrap it behind the warp strings.

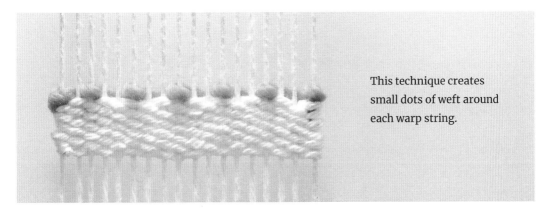

This technique creates small dots of weft around each warp string.

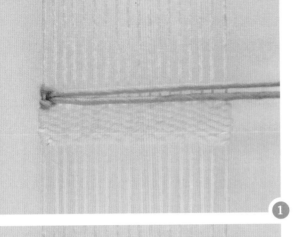

Double Soumak

Level: Beginner | Projects: Geometric Tapestry, p. 122

You can create a chevron effect and save time by weaving two tails at once for a double-soumak technique.

1. To create a double soumak, cut an extra-long length of yarn and find the center to tie it onto the first string by using a larkshead knot. You now have two separate long tails, one on top and one on bottom.

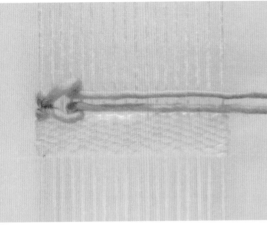

2. Working with the same method as regular soumak, use your fingers to wrap both of the tails in front of two to four warp strings and then pull them backward, up through the center of the two warp strings, as well as the center of the two tails before continuing.

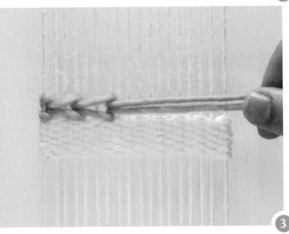

3. This is a quicker way to add two rows of soumak, but the effect will be uniform instead of overlapping.

4. The double wraps add a lot of bulk, so this technique looks best pushed tightly together.

Rya

Create bundles of equal lengths beforehand, so you are ready to add them as rya.

Have you been wondering how to add fringe and texture to the surface of your tapestry? The answer lies in the rya knot. Rya ("ree-yah") is a technique to wrap tails of yarn around the warp strings and let them hang without further weaving.

Fringe Rya

Level: Beginner | Projects: Almost All

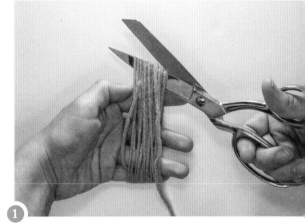

① Begin by precutting bundles of yarn. An easy way to save time is to wrap yarn around a book, a piece of cardboard, or your fingers, depending on your desired length

② Cut the bundle for a pile of equal lengths. A good amount is to have two pieces of yarn per pair of warp strings.

85

3 Create the rya knot by grabbing two lengths of yarn and placing their centers horizontally across a pair of warp strings. Now wrap the tails of your yarn around the back and up through the center of the warp strings.

4 Pull them down to stay in place and repeat with the next pair. Remember that you are weaving upside down, so the rya will appear differently when you flip your loom right side up at the end.

5 After each row of rya, complete at least one full pass (two rows) of tabby and beat it down to hold the knots in place. The rya will cover up this supporting row when your tapestry is hung up, so it is up to you how many rows to weave between the rows of knots.

6 When your tapestry is completed, you can flip the rya right side up and gently comb it out.

Because fringe rya is left long and flowing, you can have fun with the shapes that you trim it in. Create angles, perfectly straight edges, or stairsteps, or let the tassels hang at their natural lengths for different effects.

Fringe rya is a great technique to use on the bottom of tapestries. It covers up the excess warp strings so that you don't have to tuck them in, and it is my favorite way to finish a design when I want movement on the bottom.

Carpeted Rya

Carpeted, or piled, rya involves the same technique as regular ghiordes knots. It is usually done by piling multiple rows of rya tightly together (still including two thin rows of tabby in between) and cutting the fringe evenly, close to the surface of the tapestry. This way the tails support each other while standing out straight, away from the tapestry, in a short, shag carpet–like effect. This length of rya allows you to view the ends of the tails straight on. It works especially well when woven in a gradient effect, which you can learn more about in *Welcome to Weaving 2*.

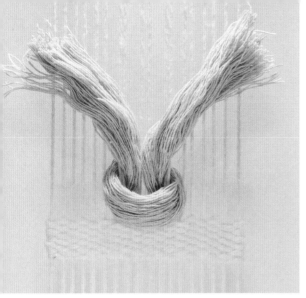

Thick Fringe

If you want your rya fringe to be extra thick and chunky, use a larger bundle of 10+ lengths at a time to wrap around four to six warp strings. One of my favorite techniques is to use thick cotton rope for my bottom rya fringe. This rope is already created from hundreds of tiny cotton threads, so when you comb out your fringe it is extra thick!

Experiment with combining different types of fringe in layers.

Hem Stitch

Level: Beginner | Projects: Almost All

The very last technique you will complete on your tapestry while it is still on the loom is also possibly the most important. It is called the hem stitch, and it will keep your weave from falling apart when you cut the warp strings free. Can you imagine all of your hard work coming apart? It could happen if you don't complete the hem stitch!

The hem stitch uses a needle and yarn to tightly pull pairs of warp strings together and hold the border in place.

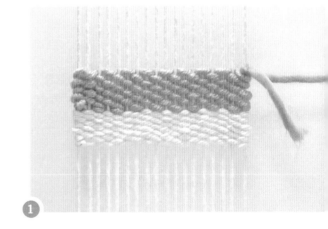

Before you begin the hem stitch, you always need at least two rows of tabby, especially if your last stitch was any type of rya. Tabby is important for the hem stitch to grab onto. You can even complete two quick rows and then go straight to working on the hem stitch with the same continuous yarn. Tie a knot on the first string and weave in the end.

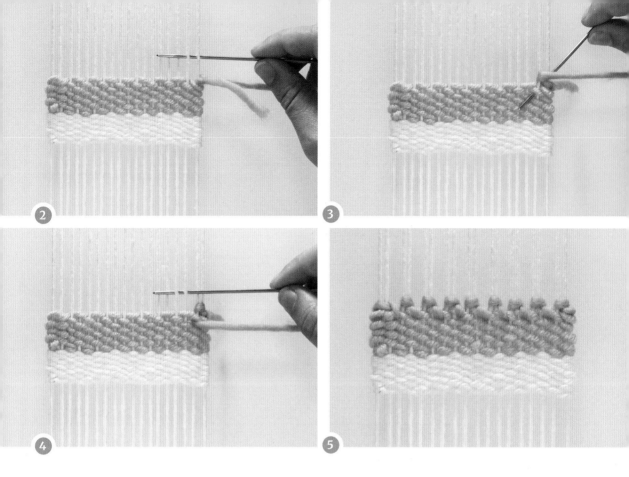

② Guide your needle behind the first two warp strings and pull the yarn through.

③ Then, guide it behind the same two warp strings, but this time come up from underneath two rows of tabby, right after the second warp string that it went behind. Pull the yarn tightly through.

④ Guide the yarn behind the next two warp strings and follow the same steps of pulling it through and then coming back up through two rows of tabby.

⑤ Continue all the way across your tapestry. Knot the end and tuck it in.

Each knot should encompass a pair of warp strings. As you pull the string under the tabby rows, the pair of warp strings is pulled tightly together. This will close up your warp so that the weft rows are held in place and won't fall down when your tapestry is cut off the loom and hung from a rod.

Open Shapes

Level: Beginner

The end isn't the only place you can use the hem stitch for stabilizing. Making open shapes with your warp strings exposed is a fun technique that seems to defy gravity. However, if you simply left an open shape and moved on, the rows at the top would sag and separate when your weave is loosened from the loom. This is where the hem stitch comes in.

(Step-by-step pictures on following page)

1. The first step is to weave around your open shape and complete your design. The hem stitch will be the last step you complete for this technique.

2. When your open shape is surrounded, use the same yarn as the edges to tuck the tail and tie a knot on the first exposed warp string.

3. Follow the steps of the hem stitch by guiding your yarn behind the first two warp strings and pulling through.
   Then guide your yarn behind the same two warp strings, this time coming up from underneath two rows of tabby.

4. Continue the hem stitch along the width of the open shape, just as you would on the bottom of the weave.

5. If you reach a vertical edge, you can sneak in a little trick of guiding your needle through a few rows of tabby, up parallel to the warp string, to easily get to the top without cutting a new length of yarn.

6. Complete the hem stitch on the other side of the open shape.

The sides of open shapes that are parallel to your warp strings will stay in place because they are selvedges and don't need any further treatment to stay strong and straight. Keep in mind that the hem stitch will add a small border as the yarn wraps around your warp strings, which could make your shape appear a bit smaller, so if the size is important to you, adjust the size of your open shape to be a tiny bit bigger than you want it to end up.

I often like to leave an entire stripe of my tapestry open, using the hem stitch for a clean, secure, and unexpected detail.

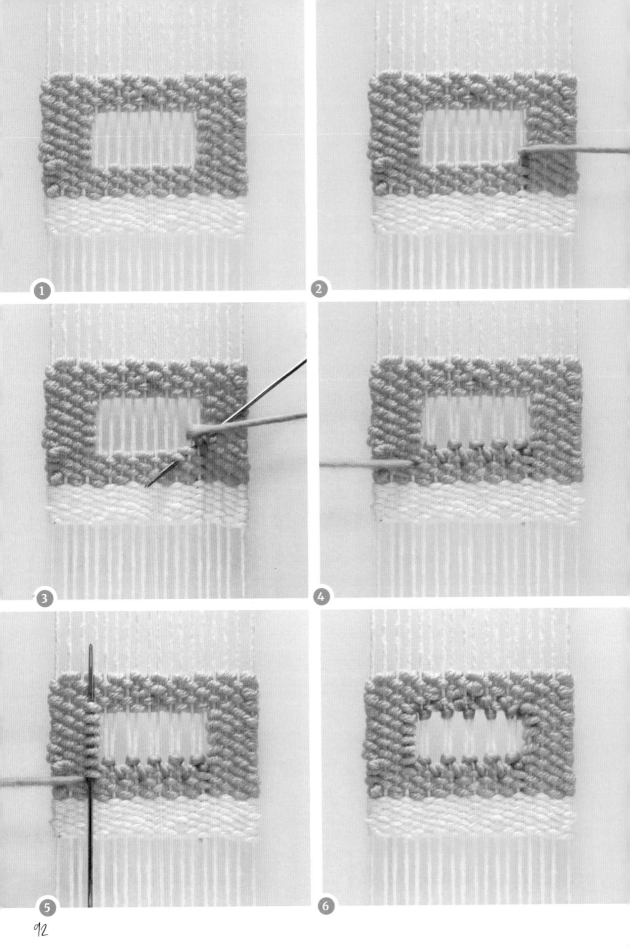

Section 4

INTERMEDIATE
TECHNIQUES

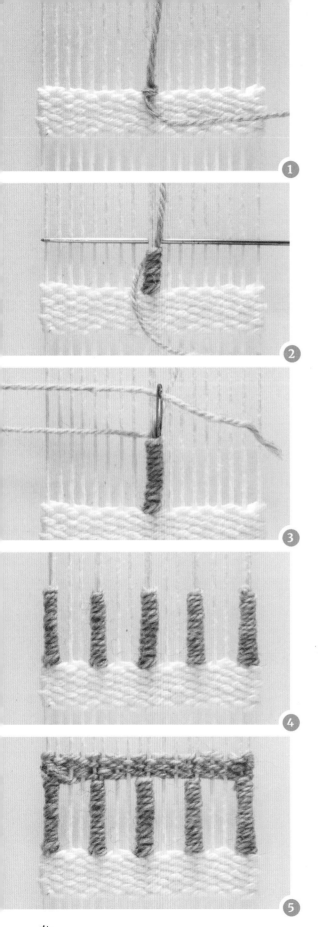

Wrapping Warps

Level: Intermediate | Projects: Basic Sampler Tapestry, p. 119

If you have chosen to leave an open space but don't like the look of your exposed warp and do want to create a bold, vertical effect, you can try wrapping your warp in a different color. When you use this method, you don't need to add the hem stitch to the tops and bottoms of the open shape because the wrapping around the warp will hold your top rows in place.

1. You can wrap around as many warp strings at once as you want, but two at a time is my recommendation. Hold a tail of the wrapping yarn parallel to your warp string, and tie a knot.

2. Begin wrapping around the bundle, starting from the bottom. Eventually you won't need to hold the tail anymore because the wrapped yarn will hold itself in place.

3. When you have wrapped as far as you want, use a needle to tuck the remaining tail parallel to the warp string bundle and out through the bottom. Cut the tail flush to the wrapped warp.

4. Continue with the next pair of warp strings if you choose. You can wrap every warp string or keep some unwrapped in between the ones you choose to wrap.

5. Add some tabby rows to the top so that you can continue weaving.

Pom-Poms and Tassels

Level: Intermediate | Projects: Extra
Embellishments Tapestry, p. 134

Pom-poms are a stylistic element that you can add to your tapestry after you have finished weaving. Pom-poms are balls of fiber that are often trimmed so that the ends face away from the center, exposing the individual materials/ colors within the tuft. You can create pom-poms solid or speckled, tightly packed or loosely packed, big or small. No matter how you create your pom-poms, they add a whimsical effect to your design.

To create a pom-pom, you need to choose something to wrap your yarn around. There are plastic, durable circle templates that you can purchase if you plan on making many pom-poms, or you can make one out of cardboard. Another method is even simpler: wrapping the yarn around your fingers.

1 Begin by holding your middle fingers together and wrapping the yarn around them 20–30 times. You can use two, three, or four fingers to alter the size of your pom and more or less yarn to determine the fullness of your pom. If you want to add speckles of different colors, simply wrap some different colors around in different spots as you wrap the main, continuous color.

2 When you are done wrapping your yarn around your fingers, cut a length about 12" long to tie around the middle. Use a needle to gently guide the yarn between your fingers and your palm on the far side of the wrapped yarn and around the yarn to the outside of your fingers to tie a quick slip knot.

3 Carefully pull the wrapped yarn off your fingers and then pull the tails of the tie so that the knot is as tight as possible. Tie a double knot to secure it in place.

4 Now, slide a pair of scissors into the loop of your yarn and cut it straight around the entire pom. Do not cut the long tails from the center knot because you will need them to hang your pom-pom onto your tapestry.

5 Fluff your pom to even out all the ends, and give it a trim to make sure it is symmetrical all the way around.

6 For a tighter, smaller pom-pom, continue trimming.

Attaching Pom-Poms

Attaching your pom-poms to the tapestry is very simple.

1. Complete a pom-pom and finish weaving the section you want to attach it to.

2. Thread a length of yarn onto your needle and guide it through the center of the pom-pom.

3. Guide the first tail through the weave.

4. Guide the second tail through the weave, a few rows/warp strings apart from the first tail.

5. Turn the weave around so that you are facing the backside, and tie the two tails together. Tuck them in and trim them.

6. You can use the tails to let your pom-pom hang if you want to add a bit of movement, or you can tie the tails tightly without excess, so that the pom-pom appears to protrude straight from the surface of your tapestry. Try combining your pom-poms next to a thick textural area such as roving, rya, soumak, or loops, so that your pom-pom partly blends in to add to the texture, or hang a cluster of pom-poms together.

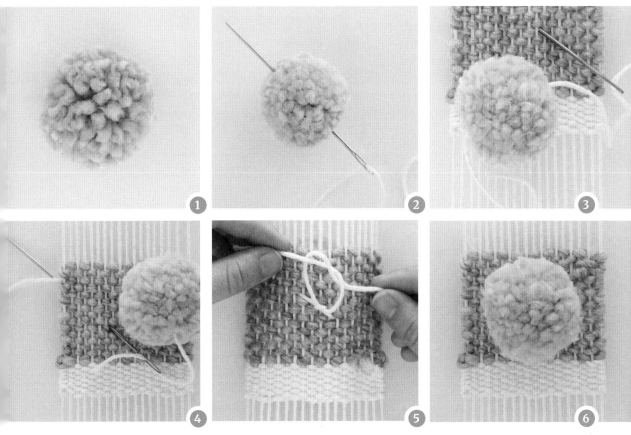

Tassels

Head-and-Skirt Tassel

Level: Intermediate | Projects: Extra
Embellishments Tapestry, p. 134

Adding tassels to a tapestry is a unique way to
incorporate some unexpected fiber embellishment. There are many ways to create tassels,
and they are easy to attach to your tapestry.

The first tassel has a basic bundle of yarn
forming the skirt, and a wrapped neck. You
can use any type of yarn, but pencil roving
will make the tassel seem fuller because the
neck can tighten around the tassel more
easily above the skirt.

1 Wrap your yarn around your hand or a
book as many times as you please,
depending on the weight of the yarn and
the size that you want for you tassel.
Here I am wrapping chunky yarn around
my hand 10–15 times. Cut a length of the
same yarn and tie it through one end of
the bundle. You can either leave the tails
from this knot out for hanging or wrap
them down among the rest of the skirt.

2 Use a gathering-knot method to wrap a
second length of yarn around the
bundle of yarn to separate the skirt
from the head and hold the tassel
together. Start with a beginning tail at
the bottom of the skirt, running up
toward the head, parallel to the bundle
of yarn that continues into a loop above
where you want the neck to be wrapped.

3 Wrap the continuous yarn tightly around the bundle of yarn to cover its own beginning tail.

4 When you reach the end of your continuous length, slip the ending tail into the loop attached to the beginning tail, which is now sticking above the wrapped neck.

5 Pull on the beginning tail to slide the loop and the ending tail below the

wrapped section. This will secure them in place. If you don't want to use the loop-and-tail method, you can tie a knot with the continuous yarn, wrap tightly around your bundle of yarn, and use a needle to guide the tail behind the neck to secure the tassel.

6 Now that the neck is in place, you can trim the bottom of your tassel skirt so that it is even.

Full-Skirt Tassel

Level: Intermediate | Projects: Extra
Embellishments Tapestry, p. 134

Depending on the material you chose to use for your first tassel, the skirt may sit straight and flat. If you are happy with this result, then tassels will be easy to re-create, but if you are disappointed that your skirt doesn't fill out wider than the neck of your tassel, there is a tassel hack to fix this problem.

1. Start by making a regular head-and-skirt tassel. Once you have the main tassel completed, begin making a second tassel with the same material. Tie the top with a thin yarn, even if it doesn't match the same material as the skirt, and leave the tails hanging. Don't wrap any yarn around to create a neck.

2. Thread the two tails hanging from the top of your tassel onto your needle, turn the first tassel upside down, and spread the yarn to find the center. Then guide the tails up through the tassel's center and out through the top of its head.

3. Tie a knot with these two tails around the tie on the main tassel's head, and then either leave them free for easy hanging or tuck them back down to hide among the skirt.

4. Trim up the bottom of your two skirts so that they are an even length. Now you have a full skirt.

Attaching Head-and-Skirt Tassels

You can attach a tassel anywhere on your tapestry. I like replacing my fringe on the bottom border with a row of tassels, or adding a prominent keyhole tassel to the front as part of the design.

To attach a regular tassel, you will need to have left tails at the top, or else just tie a new piece of yarn through the head to create new tails.

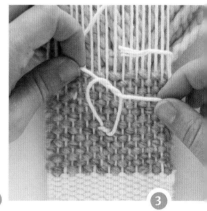

1 Thread the first tail onto your needle and pull it through your completed weave.
   Now pull the needle and tail up through a few rows of weft, parallel to the warp string, and exit out the back of the tapestry.

2 Thread the second tail onto your needle and through the completed weave. Then pull it up through a few rows of weft so that it exits at least a few centimeters apart from the first tail.

3 Turn the weave around so that you are facing the backside and knot the two tails together, then tuck the tails in.

The same method works for regular or full tassels, whether you want to add them to the middle or bottom of your tapestry.

Keyhole Tassel

Level: **Intermediate** | Projects: Extra
Embellishments Tapestry, p. 134

This tassel is called a keyhole tassel because it
has a large eye as the head with a straight skirt,
so it resembles a keyhole. You can use a bundle
of yarn, but I like to make this tassel extra easy
by substituting rope for my skirt.

1. To begin, cut a length of rope that is
   double the length that you want your
   finished tassel to be. Choose a yarn that
   you want to appear as the head, and
   begin tightly winding it around the
   rope so that the rope doesn't show
   through. The wrapped section of the
   rope should cover the middle third of
   your rope length. Tuck the end of your
   continuous yarn and then grab another
   length, either of the same yarn or a different color.

2. Fold the rope in half.

3. You can use the gathering-knot
   method or a simple knot and needle to
   wrap yarn around both tails of the
   folded rope to cover the ends of the
   wrapped head. When you reach the end
   of your yarn, tuck the tail down and cut
   it flush so that you can't see the tail.

4. You can leave your keyhole tassel with
   the two tails of rope still wound, or you
   can unwind each side and comb out the
   fringe for a blended skirt.

Attaching Keyhole Tassels

You can use a similar method to attach a keyhole tassel to the bottom of your tapestry so that it hangs from the edge, or you can attach it so that the head lies flush to the surface of your tapestry. My personal favorite is the second option.

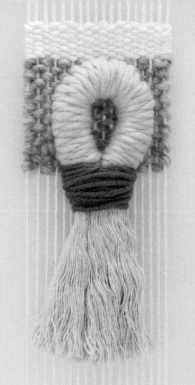

1 To secure a keyhole tassel onto the surface of your tapestry, hold it in place and use the same yarn that is wrapped around the head to sew a few loops.

2 Come up from underneath the center of the perimeter of the head and pull it tightly back down on the outside of the head, through the tapestry so that the stitches are hidden.

3 Turn the weave around so that you are facing the backside and knot the two tails together, then tuck the tails in.

Your keyhole tassel is attached flush to the surface of your tapestry, but because you used the same yarn that the head is wrapped in, you can't see any stitches!

Pom-Pom Tassel

Level: Intermediate | Projects: Basket Wrap, p. 144

Did you know that you can also create a combination of a pom-pom with a tassel? This simple trick creates a fun effect that proves that the two together are even better than one alone.

1 For this technique you will need to create one pom-pom, the bigger and fluffier the better, and one tassel. Do not tie a neck around the tassel head. Leave the ties on the top of the tassel loose.

2 Guide these ties from the top of the tassel up through the center of the pom-pom, and tie a knot to attach the tassel to the pom-pom. That's it!

3 The tassel will appear to be growing from the bottom of the pom-pom, straight out of the center. You can then use the tails from the center tie of the pom-pom to attach the pom-pom and tassel combination to your tapestry just as you would with a normal pom-pom.

Adding Embellishments

Although there are so many different types of fibrous materials that you can use in your tapestries, you can also add nonfiber embellishments. Find pieces that have a special meaning to you, and build your design around them to enrich the story behind your tapestry. If the embellishment reminds you of someone you love, a meaningful place, or a special event, your tapestry will also have more meaning as it hangs in your home.

Beads

Level: Beginning to Intermediate

One of my favorite embellishments is beads. Beads can be any type of bauble with a hole or a loop for easy hanging, including pendants, charms, lockets, sequins, and more. I enjoy searching for vintage beads and charms from around the world in many mediums, including wood, ceramics, and metal.

When you include beads, pay attention to the design of your tapestry. Depending on the size and quantity of your beads, you can use them either as an important element in the focal point of your tapestry, or as small embellishments placed throughout the fibers.

Before you begin weaving, consider if your bead is important enough to design the tapestry around it, or if your design is the star and you want the beads to work into it as an afterthought.

PENDANT BEADS

1. Some beads have a hole drilled through at some point, or a loop extending out. These are simple to attach to the surface of your tapestry with just a needle and a thread.

2. You will need to complete the fiber element of your tapestry first before sewing on your beads.

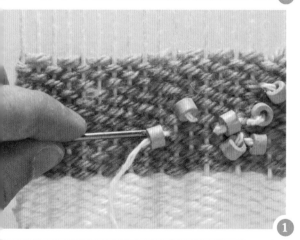

CLUSTER BEADS

1. You can also use a needle and thread to sew several small beads together in a group along the outlines of a shape or among rya loops.

2. Cluster them in an organized shape or randomly.

TWINING BEADS

Level: Intermediate | Projects: Extra
Embellishments Tapestry, p. 134

If the beads are small enough to fit between
your warp strings, you can add them while you
are weaving with the twining technique.

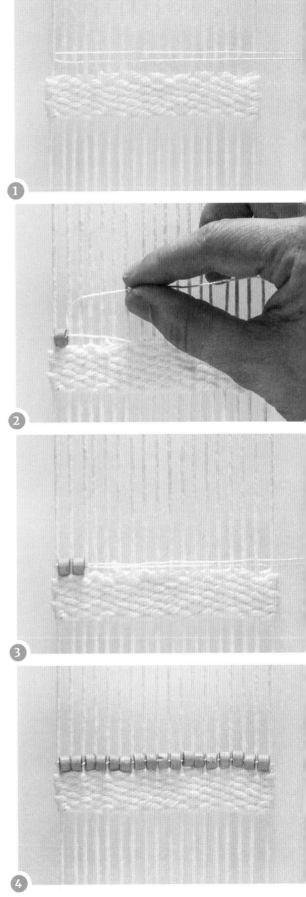

1. Use a thin but strong beading thread.
   Fold the length in half and wrap the
   half around the first warp string.

2. Slide a bead onto both tails. Keep track
   of which tail was on the bottom so that
   you can wrap it over the top tail and
   behind the next warp string.

3. Continue adding beads after each warp
   string, twining regularly along the
   length of the tapestry.

4. The beads will be organized in a row,
   flush to the surface of your weave.

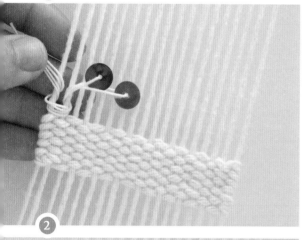

Sequins

Level: Intermediate

Loose sequins can be sewn on flush to the surface of your tapestry, or you can hang them from lengths of string to provide some movement. Sequins and metal and glass beads are beautiful when the sun hits them, and they reflect light along the walls surrounding your tapestry.

❶ Begin by stringing your sequins onto a thin string, at least 4–6" long. You can thread a bunch of sequins on the spool and then, one by one, pull them to the end of the string and cut a length.

❷ Fold the sequin lengths in half, with the sequin in the center fold. Using two at a time, wrap them onto the warp using a rya knot, so that the tails wrap behind the two warp strings up through the center.

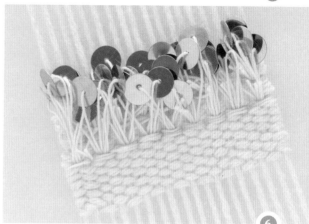

3 Continue a row of rya sequins.

4 As with all rya, always follow with a row or two of tabby.

5 Once the rya is beaten down tightly in place, you can use scissors to trim the excess tails (without sequins) to ¼" long.

6 The sequins will be securely attached to your tapestry, as long as the tabby is beaten down tightly. Experiment with longer lengths of sequins with more movement.

Fabric

Level: Intermediate | Projects: Extra Embellishments Tapestry, p. 134

Woven tapestries can be combined with other materials in some very unconventional ways. If there is an embellishment you are curious about using, chances are you can find a way to use it in conjunction with your tapestry. I challenged myself to include large pieces of prewoven fabric on the front of some tapestries because I loved the look of vintage African mud cloth with woven yarn and thick fringe. If you have a beautiful piece of fabric that you would like to include somewhere on the surface of your tapestry, there is an easy way to do this.

The first step is to cut your fabric into the shape that you want it to be on your tapestry. Once your fabric is cut, use it as a template to weave the same shape on your loom. Yes, this backing will get covered up, so use a color/material of yarn that you don't mind getting rid of. I've found that

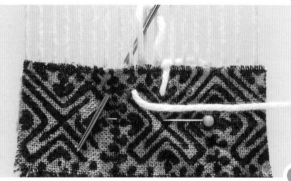

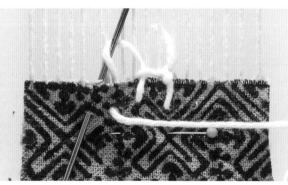

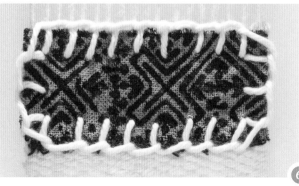

it's easier to add the fabric after all of your rows are in place instead of trying to work around the attached fabric.

2 When you are ready to add your fabric, lay it on top of the woven backing and pin it in place.

3 I prefer to attach it around the edges using a *blanket stitch*. You can use thread/yarn that is the same color as the fabric for minimal contrast. Tie a knot onto a warp string to hold the stitch in place and tuck the tail. Guide your needle up through the back of the tapestry, about ½" from the edge of the fabric. Before pulling the thread tight, guide your needle back through the loop that is created before pushing it up through the back of the tapestry again.

4 Guide your needle through each loop and up the back of the tapestry each time as you move across the length of the fabric.

5 Continue along the entire perimeter of the fabric. If you run out of thread, use the weaver's knot to add more and tuck the tails.

6 Tie a knot on the end and tuck the tails.

Leather and Other Thick Embellishments

Level: Intermediate

Thick, flat materials such as leather can be incorporated into you tapestry as well. Depending on the thickness, you may be able to sew it on the same way you would with fabric, but if it is too thick to poke your needle through, another option is to hold it in place by weaving it among the warp strings. This same method can be used with other thick elements from nature, such as leaves or feathers.

A word of caution about using thick pieces of leather. They can make your tension tighter and more brittle because they don't have the same elasticity that yarn has to help your warp bounce back where it is interconnected. They also cannot be knotted to secure themselves to the warp, so their placement can be fragile. Instead, you must build rows of yarn around their shape to suspend them in place within the shed of your warp.

1. The first step is to plan where you want to place your thick embellishment. I don't recommend drawing the shape of your object on the warp, because it won't be covered with yarn and will be easy to spot on your strings.

2. Pay attention to the shape by placing it against the loom every once in a while, as you build up your rows below where it will be held.

3. When your rows mimic the shape and angle of the bottom of the object, weave it into place within the shed of your warp and then proceed to weave rows around the side and top of the object.

4. Fill in the top of the embellishment with tabby to hold it in place. Depending on the thickness of your embellishment, it may be difficult to tightly pack your rows around it. This is natural, so just do your best to provide stability to hold the item in place.

If you place these embellishments on the outer edges of your warp so that they partly protrude past the edge, they can provide interesting composition to your tapestry by extending its boundaries beyond where you can weave.

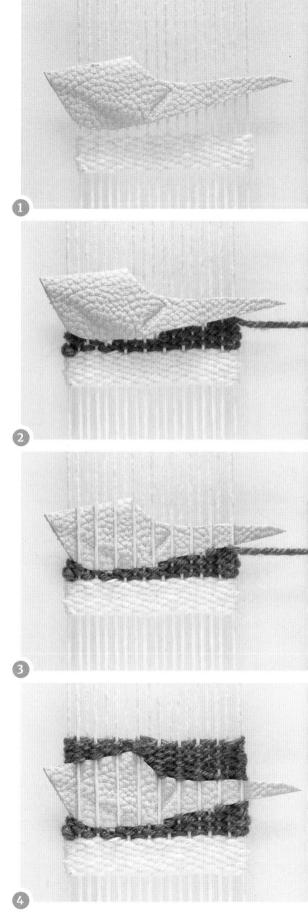

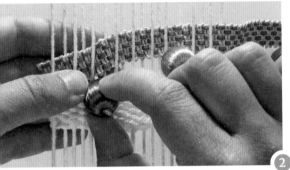

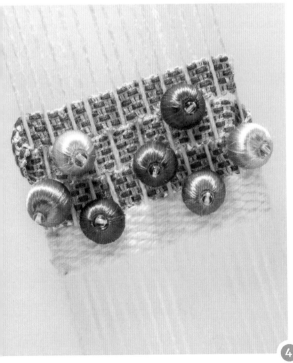

Trim

Level: Beginner | Projects: Extra
Embellishments Tapestry, p 134

Trim is a popular embellishment to weave
with because it is an easy way to add varied
texture and movement, based on what the
trim is made out of. It is a fabric-like material
that has different elements either sewn onto
the surface or hung from the bottom, such as
pom-poms, fringe, or sequins. It acts similar
to yarn because it is usually woven, so it can
be bent into rows and angles throughout your
tapestry. You can find lots of different trim in
the sewing section of your local craft store.

If your trim has extensions hanging from the
bottom, it will easily stay in place because the
extensions will be held between the warp strings
and stop the trim from coming undone. If your
trim has embellishments sewn onto the surface,
such as sequins or beads, the edges of these will
also help hold it in place among the warp strings.

1. Open your shed and place the trim in
   place.

2. If there are any extensions, pull them
   out between the warp strings.

3. If you want to stack more than one row
   of trim for a layered effect, you can
   simply open the shed again and continue
   to weave with the continuous trim. Or
   cut it at the end of the row, weave a few
   rows with plain yarn, and cut a new
   length of trim to stack above them.

4. Trim is not as flexible as yarn, but it
   adds an easy pop of pattern, color, and
   embellishment to your tapestry.

Gold Leaf

Level: Intermediate | Projects: Extra Embellishments Tapestry, p. 134

Gold leaf is another way to add some sparkle and glimmer to your work. However, unlike other embellishments, you cannot sew it on or weave it into your tapestry. Instead, gold leaf must be adhered onto the surface of your weave after the rest of the design has been completed.

You can find gold leaf at your local craft store. It comes in sheets or in small confetti-like pieces; either one works just fine.

Gold leaf works best when it is adhered to a flatter, smoother-textured surface. If your fibers are too loose, the flyaways will stop the gold leaf from sticking to your weave and it can flake off very easily.

1. The first step is to prepare a surface for your weave to sit on that can be easily cleaned. It doesn't matter if you add gold leaf while your tapestry is on the loom, or after it is cut off, but gold leaf tends to make a mess, so keep that in mind.

2. You will need a paintbrush, some tacky glue, and the gold leaf. Gold leaf adheres only to areas that are sticky from glue, so you don't need to worry about taping off the parts of your weave that you don't want gold leaf to stick to.

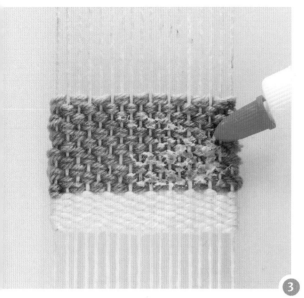

Once you have decided where you want your gold leaf on your tapestry, apply a tacky glue to that area. Any type should work as long as it stays sticky for a minute or two. Do not use superglue because it dries too quickly and it's harder to work with.

3

Wait for the glue to get tacky, about one minute, and then use a clean paintbrush to gently pick up pieces of gold leaf and firmly stick it onto the glued areas.

4

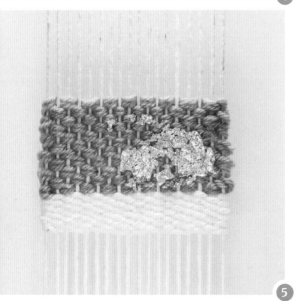

When you have covered the area that you want to include gold leaf on, wait for the glue to dry completely and then use another clean paintbrush to gently brush away any excess gold leaf.

5

Section 5
THE TAPESTRIES

Ready to put your new skills to work? In this section you will find a few tapestry designs to follow, using the techniques in previous parts of the book. You can follow along to make each one with the instructions, or mix and match the techniques to make something up yourself. The yarn you use will be different than my own collection, so feel free to play along by choosing a weight similar to what I am using, or experiment with something much different. Each design has a level of difficulty ranging from easy to hard, and labels to show which techniques were used. You can refer back to the techniques' instructions in Sections 3 and 4.

The
Practice
Tapestry

TECHNIQUES

Tabby, p. 39 | Floating Tabby, p. 66
Hem Stitch, p. 89

The practice piece is the simplest design and will help you master the basic plain weave and keeping your tension even.

Keep this tapestry small by adding only 15–20 warp strings on your loom.

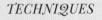 As with every tapestry, add a twining row about 1" from the bottom loops of your warp.

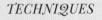 Tie a knot at the beginning warp string and use the plain tabby technique to weave 10 rows with the

first yarn. Don't forget to bubble and beat down each row to keep the tension even.

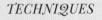 When you want to switch colors, you can either use the weaver's knot to join the two colors, or tuck the ends of

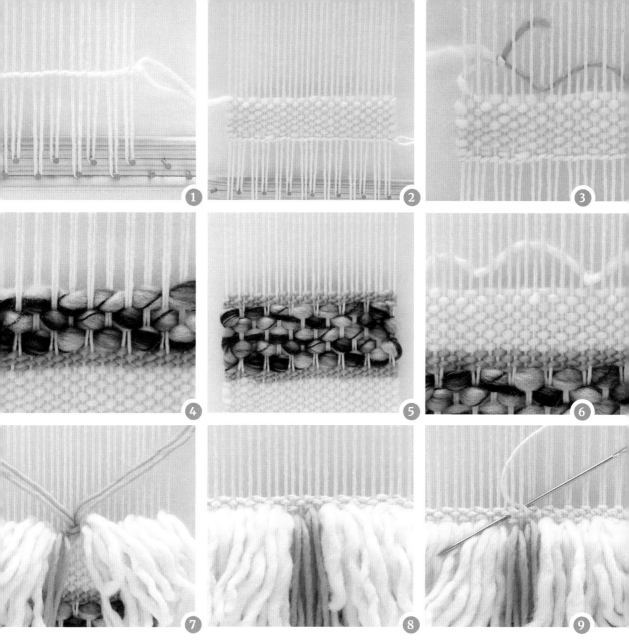

the first color and tie a knot to begin
the second color. Weave three to four
rows with the next color.

④ When you switch colors again, try
using a thicker weight of yarn for the
middle section. Instead of weaving
over and under every warp string,
practice the floating tabby by weaving
over and under two warp strings every
time. As always, don't forget to bubble
and beat for even tension.

⑤ Use the second color to weave another
three to four rows.

⑥ Use the first color to complete the
pattern with 10 rows.

⑦ Add a row of rya for the fringe.

⑧ Add two rows of tabby to lock the rya in
place, and to prepare a foundation for
the finishing hem stitch.

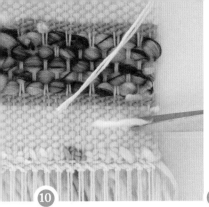

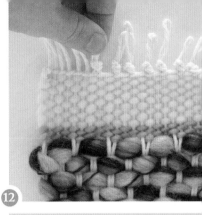

10

11

12

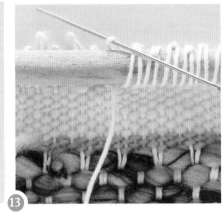

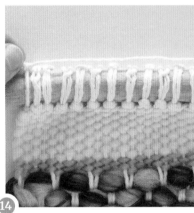

13

14

Tips

Don't forget bubbling so that your sides stay straight.

9 Tie a knot on the last warp string and add one row of the hem stitch onto the end of the tapestry.

10 Now that your practice tapestry is complete, make sure that all the ends are tucked in, and the tails on the back are trimmed.

11 Cut the warp strings above the hem stitch, leaving as much length as you prefer.

12 Complete your tapestry by tying overhand knots on each loop at the top.

13 Sew the rod onto a stick.

14 Add a hanger, if you choose.

The Basic Sampler Tapestry

The basic sampler combines a mix of techniques that are perfect for beginners. Even though each technique takes time, the mix offers good practice and results in a gorgeous home decor piece.

1. Decide how long you want your tapestry to be, warp your loom, and add a twining header row. This bottom row will be on the left side of your finished tapestry.

2. Using a thin pencil roving, weave five rows of tabby. Don't forget to bubble and beat down the rows.

3. Create horizontal stripes by alternating between two rows of different colors.

4. Move on to adding a row of triangles. Count the warp strings you have, and divide them into an equal number so that all your triangles are the same size.

5. Go through and fill in the spaces between the triangles.

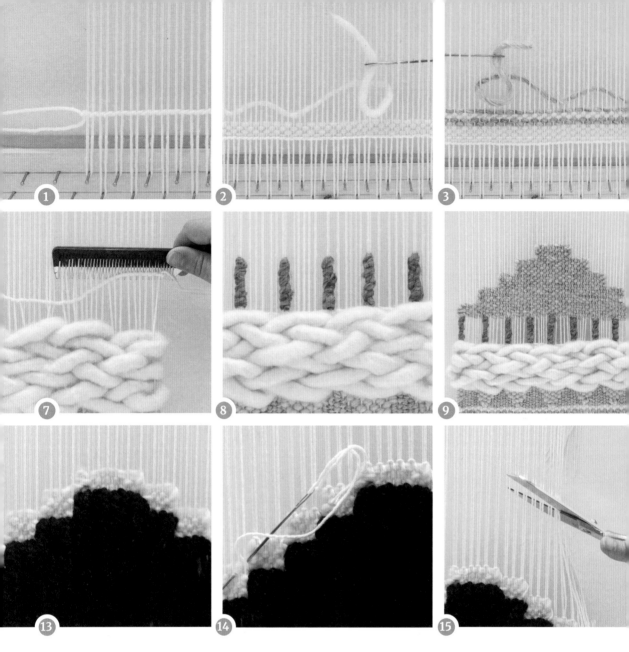

6 Use an extra-chunky yarn or roving to add five to six rows of soumak. The farther apart the loops are, the larger your braids will appear to be.

7 Soumak usually messes up the order of your warp strings, so add a twining row and beat it down, underneath the soumak, to help your warp strings line back up.

8 Wrap every few pairs of warp strings for an open element in your weave.

9 Use the plain tabby weave to weave a large stairstep area. Each section will have five to six rows of equal length before moving on to a shorter row length, until the rows finish at the top center.

10 You will be adding two rows of fringe to this piece. Add the first row by cutting one 8" long piece of yarn for every warp string you have. Add the rya to the stairsteps two at a time.

11 Add a few rows of tabby above the rya

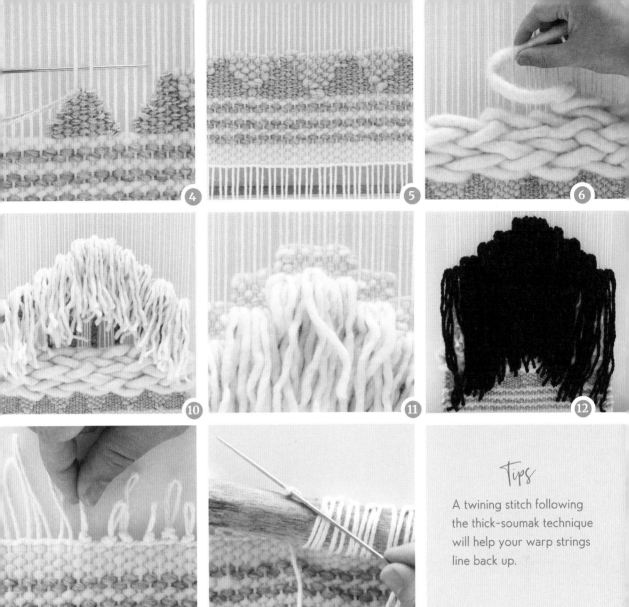

Tips

A twining stitch following the thick-soumak technique will help your warp strings line back up.

row to lock the fringe in place. The tabby will mimic the stairstep effect. The more rows you add, the farther away the second row of rya will be.

⑫ Add a second row of rya, using the same instructions from the first row.

⑬ Add another few rows of tabby above the rya row, mimicking the stairstep effect.

⑭ Finish with the hem stitch across the entire bottom border.

⑮ Turn the loom over and make sure all of your tails are tucked in, and all of your ends are cut. Cut the tapestry off the loom. The warp strings at the bottom will be covered by fringe so you can leave them free.

⑯ Use the overhand knot to tie each loop at the top.

⑰ Facing the backside of the tapestry, use the sew-on method to attach a rod to the top of the tapestry.

The
Geometric
Tapestry

TECHNIQUES

Pick and Pick, p. 67 | Shapes, p. 75
Double Soumak, p. 84 | Rya, p. 85
Stripes, p. 68 | Hem Stitch, p. 89

Test your geometry skills with a tapestry full of shapes. Even simple shapes can make a big impact in bold, bright colors.

1. Decide how wide you want your tapestry, warp your loom, and add a twining header row.

2. The most challenging part of this tapestry is right at the start! Divide the number of warp strings into two to three sections to allow for equal triangles, and use the pick-and-pick method to create triangles with vertical stripes. Each stairstep for each triangle will be two warp strings fewer than the row before.

3. Go back and fill in the space between the triangles with tabby.

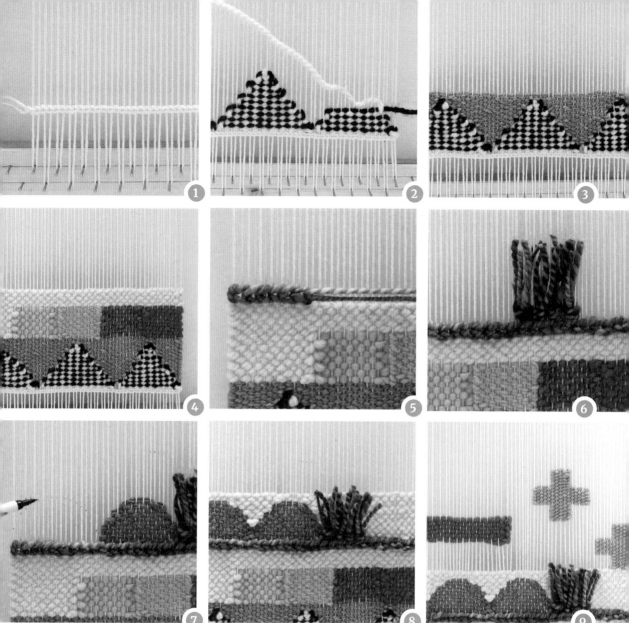

④ Divide your warp strings into smaller equal parts and add a row of blocks. Their sides can be connected however you want, but here they are straight split. Add a few rows of tabby above the blocks.

⑤ Fold a length of yarn in half and use the tails to add a double-soumak row.

⑥ Add a patch of long, skinny rya tassels if you want that type of texture in this piece.

⑦ Draw an outline of half circles next to the rya and fill them in.

⑧ Fill in the space between the half circles and after the rya.

⑨ Add any other shapes that you want to include, such as blocks or crosses.

⑩ Fill in the spaces between these shapes with rows of tabby. As you come underneath a shape, you will have less

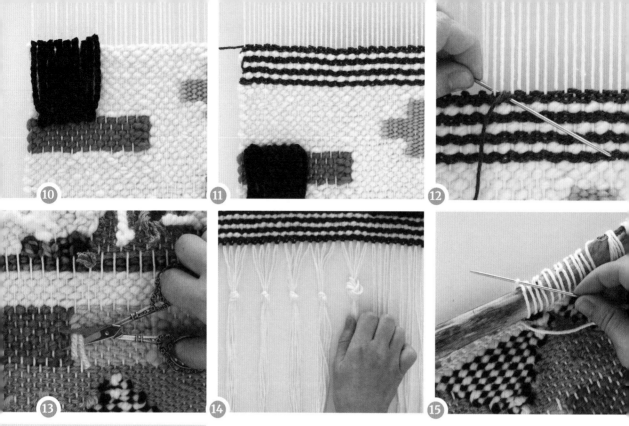

Tips

Create your shapes first and then fill in around them with tabby. A solid background makes shapes pop.

space to weave, so a weaving needle comes in handy! Add another patch of rya if you want.

11 Add four to five alternating rows of different colors for a striped border at the end of the tapestry.

12 Use the same color as the last tabby row you wove to add a row of hem stitch.

13 Turn the tapestry over to the backside and make sure all the tails are tucked in, then trim any ends.

14 Cut the warp strings as long as you can, and use an overhand knot to knot equal bundles together.

15 Use the overhand knot at the top of the tapestry loops. Then use the sew on method to attach a stick or rod.

The Full–Fringe Tapestry

By using layers upon layers of rya you can create 3-D shapes out of fringe. Experiment with different ways to cut the fringe for a waterfall effect or a modern take on a grassy landscape.

1. Decide how wide you want your tapestry, warp your loom, and add a twining header row.

2. Add six rows of tabby. Don't forget to bubble and beat them down!

3. Use a felt-tip marker to draw outlines of general shapes on your warp.

4. Cut bundles of yarn. It helps if you already have an idea about where you want to place them and how long you want them to be in the end, so that you can cut some colors shorter or longer based on what you need.

5. Work on the first row. Add bundles of yarn using the rya knot. When you come to the end of a shape, switch colors.

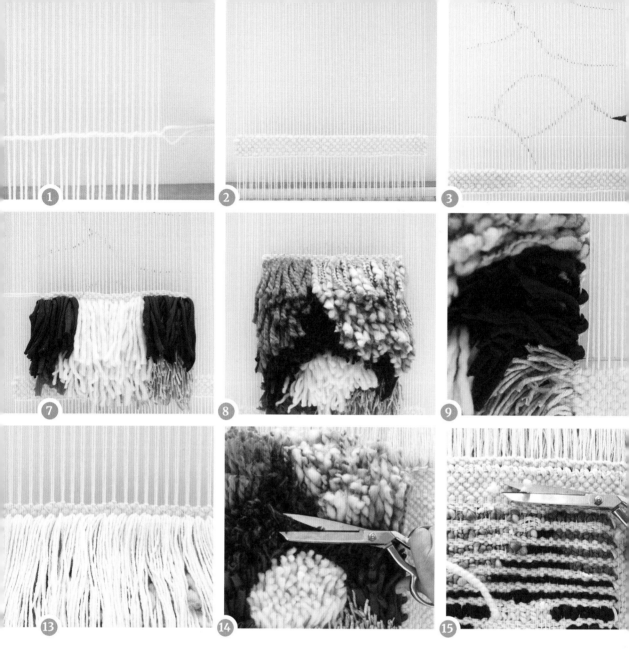

6 After each row, add a few rows of plain tabby to lock the rya in place.

7 Continue working row by row, alternating between rya and tabby. Remember, you are weaving upside down, so the fringe will look a bit different when you flip the tapestry over at the end.

8 Finish the rows of rya shapes. The edges both of the rya and tabby should end on the same warp string for a long, straight split border on either side.

9 Go back to the right side and begin adding rows of tabby to frame the fringe. Use the dovetail technique to connect each row of tabby to the border of fringe.

10 Repeat the tabby rows on the other side and then along the top for an equal border all the way around the fringe.

11 Add a single row of fringe, the same color as the border tabby, along the entire width of the tapestry.

(4)

(5)

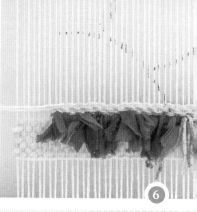

(6)

(10)

(11)

(12)

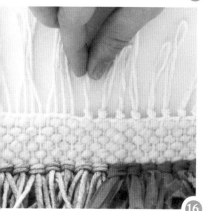

(16)

(17)

Tips

Always add a consistent number of tabby rows after each row of rya to keep the fringe separations consistent.

12 Add at least two tabby rows to prepare for the hem stitch and lock the rya in place.

13 Add a row of hem stitch along the border.

14 While the warp strings are still taut on the loom, trim your rya shapes so that some are shorter or longer than others.

15 Turn the tapestry around to the backside and make sure all the tails are tucked in, then trim any extras. Cut the

warp strings at the end to remove the tapestry from the loom.

16 Use the overhand knot to tie each warp loop at the top.

17 Sew the stick or rod onto the top of the tapestry.

The
Sideways
Weave
Tapestry

By now you probably know that weaving rules are made to be broken. Experimenting with the techniques leads to some unexpected results, such as sideways weaving! Sideways weaving is created on a frame loom with regular warp and weft; however, when it is removed from the loom it is turned on its side so that the weft points vertically and the warp holds it together horizontally.

This project is a great way to experiment with your techniques using new eyes, because instead of lying horizontally, the elements of the weaving will lie vertically when the tapestry is completed. A small change in direction can completely change the effect of a technique!

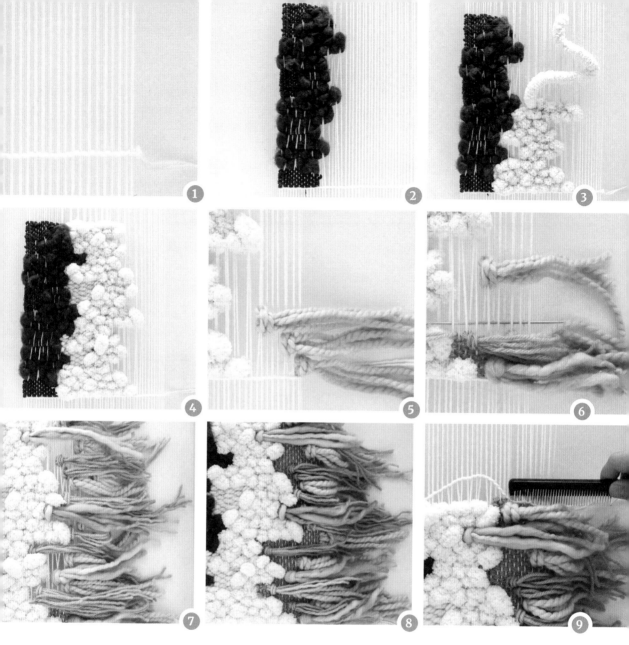

1 Decide how long you want your tapestry to be, warp your loom, and add a twining header row. This bottom row will be on the left side of your finished tapestry.

2 Begin the top of your tapestry design by working on a free-form column on the left side of the loom. The length of your column will be the width of your finished tapestry.

3 Working with columns instead of rows means some rows may be longer than others. Make sure the columns connect either by hatching, interlocking, or joining.

4 Here the free-form rows are being connected with hatching.

5 When you want to add some fringe to the bottom, use a dovetail knot instead of rya, so that the fringe faces sideways.

Tips

The side will be your bottom. This may be obvious, but keeping this flip in mind will help your design. Do you still want fringe to border the bottom? If so, you will need to add fringe along the side of your tapestry as you are weaving. If you want any designs to be at the top of your tapestry, you will need to design them on the sides, and vice versa.

6 Fill in around the dovetail fringe with tabby rows to connect the supporting warp string to the rest of the warp strings around it for support. If you don't, your warp string will sag from the weight of supporting all the fringe.

7 You can add dovetails to different warp strings for a layered fringe look.

8 Be sure to fill all the fringe in with tabby. Some tabby will be on the right and left of the knots as well as on top and on bottom to make sure it is packed in. The last warp string on your right will be the very bottom of the tapestry.

9 Add a twining row at the top of the design and comb it straight. This top row will be on the right side of your finished tapestry.

10 Cut your tapestry off the loom.

11 Turn the tapestry over and make sure that all the tails are trimmed. You can tuck in the side warp strings for a clean edge, or let them hang for extra fringe on either side.

12 Sew the top of your tapestry onto a rod. Use a needle to guide your string below the top warp string and around the rod, tying a knot on either end and tucking the tail.

The Circular Star Weave Tapestry

TECHNIQUES

Tabby, p. 39
Triangles, p. 78
Soumak, p. 82

Although weaving is limited to the confines of your loom, that doesn't mean that you can't get creative with what you use as your loom. Square looms might be the norm, but looms come in lots of shapes, such as triangles and circles. Weaving on a circle is quick and easy. Many stitches are continuous as you go around, so you don't even have to turn around to create the next row. On a circular loom you can use almost every single technique that you can on a regular loom. Have fun experimenting and translating your style of weaving to this new shape.

1. Begin by wrapping your metal hoop with yarn, fabric, or leather so that your warp string will stay in place as you pull it around the hoop. It is helpful to use superglue to adhere the yarn in a few places on the metal as you wrap it tightly around the entire hoop.

2. Wrap the entire hoop.

3. To warp a circular tapestry, begin as you would with a regular warp by tying the end onto the top middle of your hoop. Pull your string down straight to the bottom middle and wrap it over the hoop from front to back.

4. Then pull it back up to the front of the top, wrapping it around to the front, 1" to the left of the starting knot.

5. Now pull it back up to the bottom again, wrapping it around to the back 1" to the right of the first bottom warp.

6. Continue doing this, working clockwise from top to bottom, always wrapping from the front to the back. As you add more warp, your center will get full of crisscrossing strings. When you have finished warping all the way around the hoop, don't tie off your last warp string just yet.

7. Pull the last warp string down around the center, where the warp strings intersect. Wrap it twice around the center, pulling all the intersections into one point from which they can radiate out. Now guide the last warp string back up to its last resting spot and tie a knot to complete the warping process. Count each time you loop your warp around the metal frame. You need an ODD number for your rows to work, so be sure to finish with an odd number only.

8. The center of your tapestry will be extra tight and unorganized. Use a thin yarn in

the center with the plain tabby weave to organize the warp strings by weaving around the center. Use your needle to push the rows tightly in place every once in a while. Because you have an odd number of warp strings, when you get to the end of your row you can just continue around the circle.

9. Add a few rows of soumak to see how the circular weave alters the effect of the braids.

10. Count the number of warp strings and divide them equally to add some triangles or other shapes. Because you are weaving in a circle, the triangles will look like a star.

11. Fill in the space between the triangles. As you get closer to the outside of your loom, the warp strings will be more spread out, so thicker materials work well.

Metal hoops are cheap and strong. You can pick one up at your local craft store to use as a loom for your circular weave. You don't have to cut the weave off the circular loom at the end—simply hang your weave up!

12. The last bit of your warp will be extra tight, so use a forgiving technique, such as soumak with a thick material, to fill in the outside.

The
Extra Embellishments
Tapestry

TECHNIQUES

Tabby, p. 39 | Trim, p. 112
Beads, p. 105 | Gold Leaf, p. 113
Fabric, p. 109 | Pom-Poms, p. 95
Tassels, p. 98 | Rya, p. 85 | Hem
Stitch, p. 89 | Dovetail, p. 49

What better way to learn to use embellishments than by putting them all in one tapestry? This piece combines trim, beads, fabric, gold leaf, pom-poms, and tassels. Try to find embellishments that harmonize in color so that this tapestry isn't too busy.

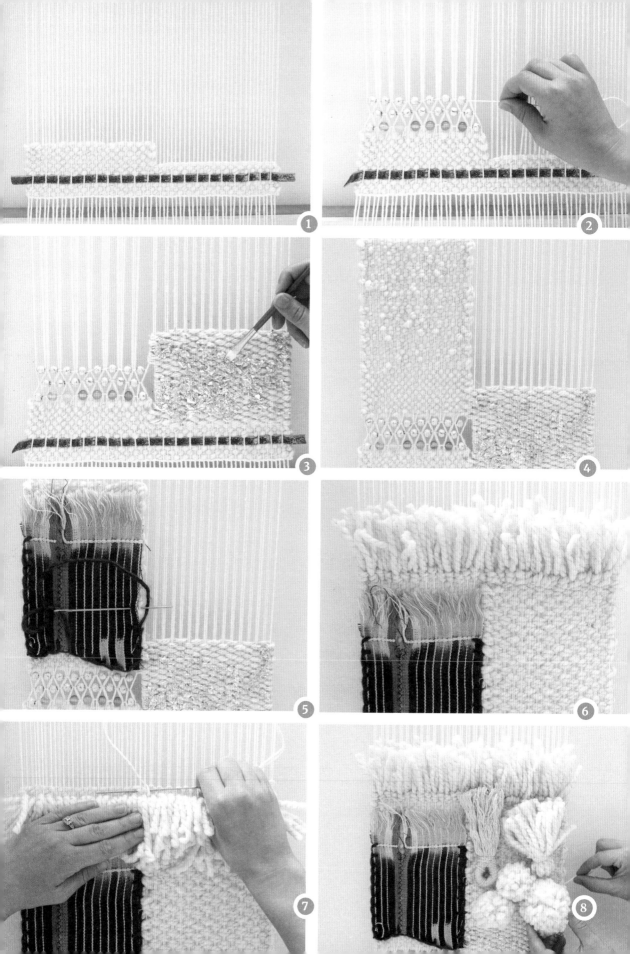

1. Add a few rows of tabby along with a row of bright, sparkling trim for a pop at the top. You can tuck the trim in the back of the tapestry or leave the edges hanging out.

2. Use a needle and thread to twine some beads within the warp strings. These beads are larger than the width between warp strings, so you can bundle some warps in between each bead for a lattice effect.

3. Complete a section of tabby and then add gold leaf. Allow the gold leaf to dry before touching it so that it stays in place.

4. Complete a column on the right of tabby, the same size as the piece of fabric you will be sewing on.

5. Use the blanket stitch to sew your fabric onto the tabby.

6. Fill the rest of the tapestry up with rows of tabby. Be sure to dovetail any sections or columns of tabby to connect the rows. Add a row of rya at the end of the tapestry, followed by a row of tabby to lock it in place.

7. Add a row of hem stitch at the end, underneath the rya.

8. Make a group of tassels and pom-poms and attach them to the surface of the tapestry.

9. Turn the tapestry over and make sure all the tails are tucked in and trimmed. Cut the tapestry off the loom.

10. Add an overhand knot to each warp loop at the top of the tapestry.

11. Sew on a rod and add a hanger.

Other Ways to Use Weaving

You've learned dozens of new techniques and practiced a handful of tapestries, but you may be wondering . . . "Is that it? Do I make tapestry after tapestry, or are there other ways to use weaving?" Of course, there are! Weaving is such a universal craft—it is practiced on every continent and has been used since the dawn of time. Now that you have the skills, it's time to think outside the box and explore the opportunities for weaving.

When you finally put down this book, I want you to feel confident that even with a small tapestry loom you can make anything you want. A loom is just a tool—not a limitation. You don't need a huge loom to make huge projects. You will notice that many of the projects are made up of two, three, even six pieces sewn together.

The projects in this section of the book are meant as ideas to jump-start your own creativity. The specifics given for each panel are less detailed than the instructions on technique in Sections 3 and 4 or the tapestry projects in Section 5, because I want you to incorporate your own materials and techniques. The instructions here focus mostly on how to take a simple woven sample and transform it into something besides a tapestry.

Mini Weave Garland

The saying "the more the merrier" definitely applies to tapestries! If one large tapestry is a special decor piece, five or six smaller tapestries can be even better, especially when they are connected on a continuous garland. This sweet project looks great in a nursery or in holiday colors over a mantel.

1 Begin by creating five to six small tapestries, each about 4" wide. You can be creative with their shape and styles so that each one is the same, or mix it up so that they all are completely different.

2 Sew the warp loops of each piece onto a long length of rope.

3 Tie the ends of the rope in a knot to keep it from fraying, and hang up your garland!

Tote Decor

Add a tapestry panel to your favorite woven or canvas bag for a personalized element that you can show off wherever you carry it.

Decide where you want to include a woven piece. It can be as a band along the top opening of the bag, or a panel to fill the entire front. Keep in mind that like pillows, bags get a lot of wear and tear from everyday use, so you want to use materials and techniques that will last as long as possible.

1. Once you have completed your tapestry to your desired size for the bag, remove it from the loom.

2. Fold the excess warp sides of your tapestry underneath to prevent them from coming undone, and pin your weave in place onto the bag.

3. Tightly sew around the borders to attach it onto your bag. Be sure not to sew any fringe down, because you will want it to hang and sway as you move the bag.

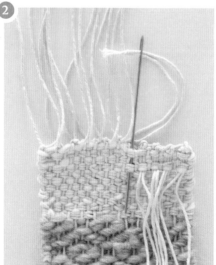

Branch Weaving

Tapestry looms come in many sizes and shapes . . . you can even find a loom ready to use in your own backyard. Branch weaving is one of the most basic forms of weaving because you simply weave within the space of a V-shaped branch, but the results can be anything but primitive. This is also a great project for kids to learn how to weave.

Branch weaving is just like weaving on a loom. The important thing is to find a good branch. You will need a branch that has a fork with a space in the center large enough to weave on. The branch will also need to be strong enough to maintain tension so that the outer branches don't bend in as they get farther from the fork. Trim any excess twigs, leaves, or smaller branches that you don't want to be included in your final tapestry.

1. To warp the branch, begin at the narrowest area, near the fork. Tie a knot and pull your string over the front of the branch to the other side. Then wrap it around to the back and over to the front of the next side again. Continue wrapping your warp in a figure-eight pattern so that every time you pull it to

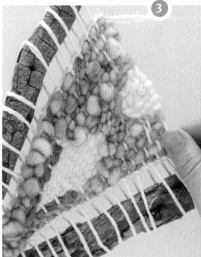

either side it gets wrapped from front to back. This will make sure that your warp meets evenly in the center, and makes it easier for your warp to lie flat among the stitches.

② Add a twining header to the top and bottom of the fork in your stick so that your warp is flat on the same plane.

③ Begin weaving normally. The tabby stitch is the easiest to do on a branch weave. The narrow end of the fork means that fewer techniques will work. However, experiment with different materials and techniques.

Necklace

I love to use weaving as wearable art by hanging small tapestries on cord and wearing them as necklaces. Easy enough for a group of kids or beginning weavers to finish in an afternoon, it is also a great gift to give, and a fun conversation piece.

❶ & ❷ Measure a loop of soft rope around your neck and lay both tails on the outer two warp strings. Begin weaving, including the outer rope in your rows to bind them in place.

❸ & ❹ Use the twining technique to add a row of beads. Add a few rows of rya in a triangle shape for fringe.

❺ & ❻ Cut the warp strings to remove your necklace from the loom. Tuck the long ends of the top warp strings into the back rows and trim the tails.

Basket Wrap

A thin panel of weaving can turn a woven basket from plain to special. You can add a handmade border along the top by using a quick, skinny tapestry hung sideways. Add fringe or pom-poms to incorporate extra texture.

1 Begin by measuring the perimeter of your basket. Since your border will need to run along the entire length of the perimeter of the basket, you will need to make sure that your tapestry is long enough.

2 If your loom is too short, you can make multiple pieces to sew together so that they add up to the needed length.

3 After the piece is cut from the loom, tuck the warp strings into the last few rows on the end of each strip and sew them together, end to end.

4 Sew the wrap around the top of your basket.

5 When you have gone all the way around the perimeter, sew the ends together.

6 Add a pom-pom tassel to the front.

Bed Runner

1

4

Extra-long woven goods are usually reserved for more-advanced looms such as rigid heddle looms or floor looms, but by now you probably know that nothing is impossible when it comes to weaving. This table / bed runner project can easily be made by sewing a few panels together. It is a great way to add texture to flat surfaces and to show off your skills during your next dinner party.

Warp your loom for low density and use chunky yarn to finish this project faster. Clusters of rya will add great texture on some of the panels. Begin and end with a twining row.

2 Design your weave with the separate panels in mind so that you know where different techniques will be positioned in the final project. For a king-size bed I made seven panels, each about 15" long.

3 Tuck the tails of all panels in.

4 Sew the panels end to end, by the twining rows.

5 Add extra lengths of tassels at the end of your bed runner if you want more fringe hanging off.

1 Begin by choosing the length and width that you want for your finished runner. You will be limited by your frame loom's dimensions, so factor in how many panels you will need to finish to create one long piece.

Pillow

Woven pillows are a popular way to display your new skills. Keep in mind that pillows are touched and used, unlike wall hangings. In order to keep them lasting as long as possible, choose materials and techniques that can withstand the extra abuse—I mean, love.

Tightly spun cotton, wool, and other natural materials are best to use because they are soft but still smooth and strong. Loose spun roving will get snagged and pulled more easily. Keep your warp strings close and your rows tight so that the stitches can't be pulled out.

1. When you have completed your tapestry to the desired size of your pillow and removed it from the loom, you don't need to attach the ends onto a rod.

2. Cut two pieces of fabric, each the same size as your tapestry panel. One will be used as the lining on the backside of your tapestry, and the other will be the back of the pillow.

3. Sandwich your tapestry in the following order: (1) backside fabric panel, right side facing up, (2) tapestry, right side facing down, (3) lining fabric panel. Now pin the three layers together.

4. Sew a straight line around the two sides, the top, and an inch or two on either side of the bottom, leaving an opening at the side.

5. Turn the pillow right side out.

6. Stuff the pillow. Sew up the opening.

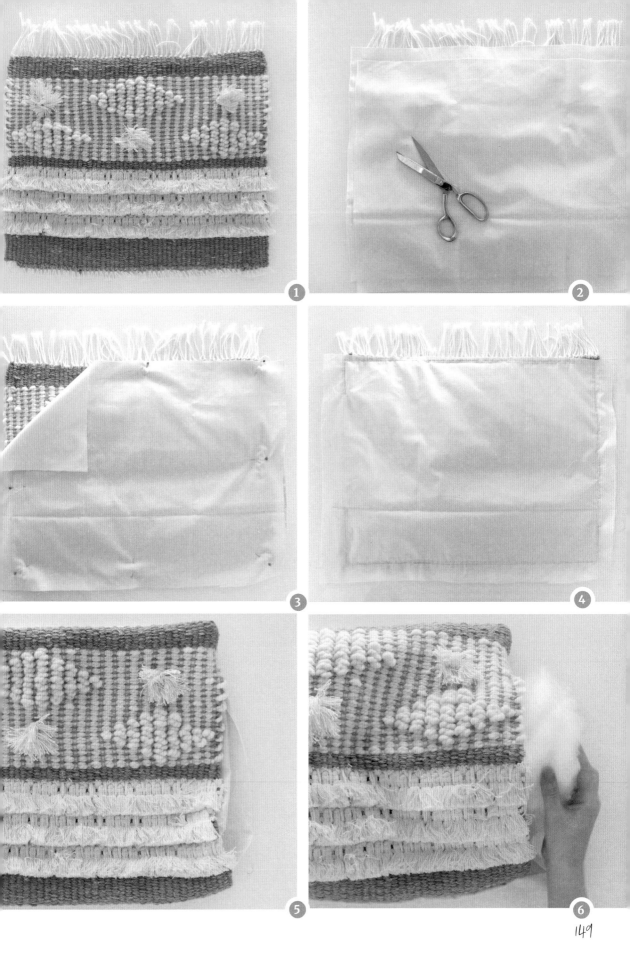

Chandelier

Create a large-scale piece to show off your skill! A woven chandelier fits the bill perfectly. This project looks best with lots of fringe and maybe even a few glass beads to sparkle in the light.

1. You will need two or three embroidery hoops in various sizes. Here I am using a 10", a 14", and an 18" hoop.

2. Measure the perimeter of each embroidery hoop. You will need to wrap a tapestry around each hoop, so make sure that width measurement will fit on your loom. If your loom isn't big enough, you can create two different panels and sew the sides together to reach all the way around.

3. For the largest hoop, cut lengths of rope and attach them by using larkshead knots to cover the wood of the hoop. The other hoops will have tapestries sewn on, so the wood will be revealed, but the tops of those hoops will be hidden behind the fringe of the outside hoop.

4. Your tapestries for this project don't have to be very long because they will hang in layers. About 3–4" is long enough, including any fringe that you want. Leave loops at the top of each tapestry.

5. Sew any panels together that need to be longer to fit around the hoop.

6. Because you left loops at the top of your tapestries, you can simply sew them onto the hoops the same way that you would with a straight rod: by wrapping the loops around the hoop and attaching them to the back.

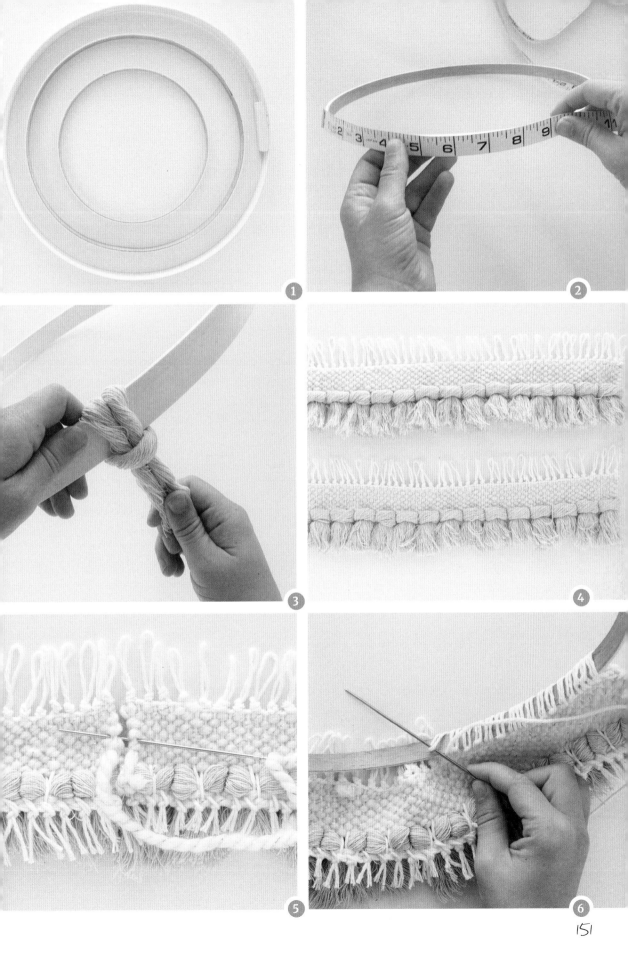

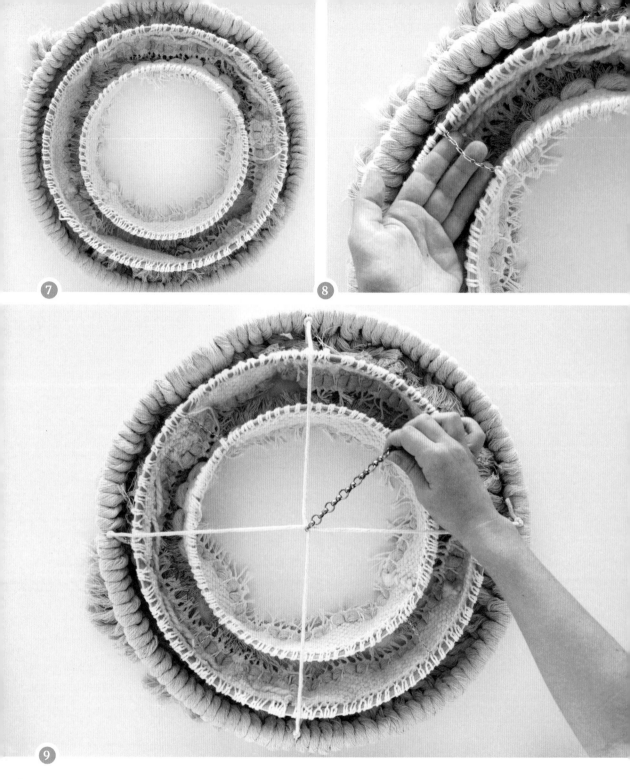

7   When all your tapestries are attached
to the hoops, place them inside each
other on a table.

8   Use four even lengths of chain per
hoop to tie the hoops inside each
other, smallest to largest.

9   Attach two even lengths of rope evenly
in four places around the largest hoop.
Attach a strong hanging chain to the
center intersection. When you hang
your chandelier up, the smaller hoops
will hang in layers below the larger
hoops, creating a three-dimensional
tapestry with lots of movement!

Section 1

CONTINUING
ON YOUR OWN

Now that you have a toolbelt full of techniques and projects to reference, I'm sure you want to pursue your own ideas! This section is my attempt to guide you onto the next path of your weaving journey as you search for inspiration to understand what will make your contribution to the weaving world unique.

Finding Inspiration

The best thing about weaving is that you can find inspiration for designs everywhere you go! Doors, furniture, tile, trees, fences, paths, piles of paper, children's toys, clothing, rocks, clouds—it doesn't even have to be a recognizable shape to inspire your tapestry.

If you want your designs to be truly unique, look for inspiration in other art mediums. Stretch your creativity by giving yourself an assignment to interpret a painting, a piece of pottery, interior design, or even a fashion show onto your loom.

Need a prompt? Go to your local grocery store and choose a bouquet or two, and use that as inspiration for your next piece!

Finding Your Style

No two weavers will create the same designs. Even when they follow the same patterns, each weaver's tapestry will look different, and that is one reason I love this craft! I think the biggest key to mastering modern weaving (besides practice, practice, practice) is to never stop experimenting. There are many ways that other weavers approach the same techniques that I have included in this book, so explore your own methods and have confidence in your style. As you continue weaving, you will find that there are certain elements you enjoy incorporating more than others. I think understanding personal preferences is an essential step to claiming a unique style.

Color

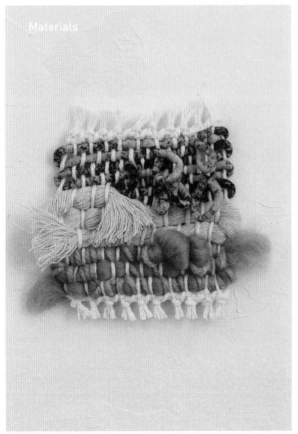

Materials

Color

Understanding and developing your weaving style involves paying attention to the colors that you choose to use. Do you like bright and colorful or subdued and monochrome? Take a glance around your home, your closet, and your Pinterest boards to pinpoint the colors that draw you in the most. Once you have found your color preference, it is much easier to choose materials and palettes that you will find most fulfilling and inspiring to use.

You might love the thickness and texture of that bright yellow yarn, but can you see yourself using the color in your own work? Selecting and combining colors is one of the best ways to stretch your creativity, so treat them like vegetables and try a new color at least once before deciding against it. You might be surprised that you actually have a taste for it!

Materials

Yarn is yarn . . . right? Absolutely not! As you continue to find your style, you will notice yourself gravitating toward different materials. Do you love the fluffiness of roving or the stiffness of rope? The more materials you get a chance to work with, the more you will appreciate the difference among them.

Challenge yourself by using an unconventional material like ripped jeans or fringe trim. You will soon notice yourself reaching for your favorite materials and searching for a specific feature like "hand spun" or "wrapped cord" over other materials that don't speak to you as much.

Embellishments

One of my favorite hobbies, second to weaving, is finding baubles and embellishments to add nonfiber features to my tapestries. I prefer vintage metal and wood charms from around the world because they add their own story to my designs. You can choose to add nonfiber embellishments to your tapestry by weaving them in as you go or by sewing them on at the end. Your personal style will determine if these pieces have a place of prominence, front and center, or if they are subtly tucked in among your stitches. Charms from your own past are a great way to make your weaves and your walls even more special.

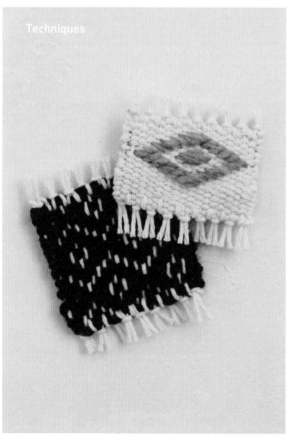

Techniques

Perhaps the number-one way to find your own style is by coming back, again and again, to your favorite techniques. It's always fun to play around with new methods (you have to try everything at least once, right?) but as your repertoire of techniques grows, you will notice which become your go-tos, so that you can create your signature look. Look at your favorite weavers to see which techniques they prefer. Some artists are known for using only one technique, such as soumak or rya, through their entire collections.

Glossary of Terms

balanced weave: Going over the same number of warp strings that you go under.

beating: Pressing a row of weft yarn into place with a beater device such as a comb.

blanket stitch: Used to attach fabric to a tapestry.

blocking: Post-weaving technique to fix puckering/bulging by using heat and steam.

blocks: Square or rectangle shapes.

Brooks bouquet: Weaving technique of wrapping bundles of warps together with a weft string.

bubbling: The act of creating hills of weft during tabby to maintain tension.

bulging: When a tapestry is cut off the loom and the warp strings expand apart due to improper tension, causing the edges or middle to curve outward.

carpeted rya: Weaving technique with rows of tightly packed rya, cut short.

circle: Shape with curved edges.

concave selvedges: Edges of a tapestry bow inward.

convex selvedges: Edges of a tapestry bow outward.

double soumak: Weaving technique of weaving two tails as soumak at once.

dovetail: Rows of weft overlap by a single warp string, alternating between short and long.

draping: Weaving technique letting yarn hang in an arch.

draw in: When the edges of the weave curve inward during weaving due to improper tension, such as the weft being too tight. See concave selvedges.

Egyptian knot: The soumak technique done backward.

epi: "Ends per inch" applies to the thickness of warp strings and how many will make up an inch when laid touching, side by side. Low epi means thinner yarn; high epi means thicker yarn.

fiber: A material used to make yarn.

flat weave: Two-dimensional weaving technique to create patterns within the surface of the weave. The weft is guided back and forth through the warp continuously.

float: A warp or weft yarn that travels over more than one adjacent warp or weft.

floating tabby: Balanced weave of tabby that goes over and under more than one warp string at a time.

free-form: Weaving freely, not constrained by rows.

full pass: Two rows of balanced tabby weave.

gaping: When a straight split does not butt up together, creating a gap in the tapestry.

ghiordes knot: The most common rya technique.

gradient: Two or more colors fading into each other.

half pass: One row of balanced tabby weave.

hanger: The piece of string at the top of a rod to hang the tapestry on the wall.

hatching: Rows of weft overlap by many warp strings, alternating between short and long.

heddle: A device using fiber leashes to pick up a pattern of warp strings at the same time so that the shuttle can easily pass through the open shed.

hem stitch: A weaving technique to end tapestries; pulls warp strings together to hold the rows above in place.

interlocking: Rows of weft join at the turn to connect a straight split.

joining: Sewing up a straight split to avoid gaping.

keyhole tassel: A tassel that has a round head with a hole in the center and a straight skirt; resembles a keyhole.

knot and slip: A technique to attach a tapestry to a rod by slipping the rod through the warp loops.

krabbasnar: A weaving technique using a single supplementary warp to build vertical columns.

larkshead knot: Folding a length of yarn in half and slipping the tails through the loop around an item.

leno: A gauze-type weaving technique that twists warps together in an open weave.

loom: A tool used to hold warp strings taut during weaving.

loop and tail: A way to tie off the neck of a tassel without using any extra tools, by pulling both tails below the neck using an attached loop of the same yarn.

looped rya: Fringe that drapes between itself.

needle: A long, thin tool with an eye to guide the weft through the shed.

notches: Nails or guides on either side of a loom to hold the warp in place.

open shapes: Areas in a weave where the warp is left visible.

overshot: A supplementary weft technique where the extra weft floats behind the width of the tapestry when it is not used on the surface.

pencil roving: A thinner, slightly spun roving.

pibione: A weaving technique creating loops of pile weave in a pattern or shape.

pick and pick: Vertical stripes created from two different-colored tabby rows.

pick-up stick / shed stick: A tool used to open the shed for faster weaving.

pile weave: A weaving technique to create loops by wrapping tabby between warp strings onto a smooth rod, such as a knitting needle.

pom-pom: A bushy, textural ball of yarn where the tails face outward.

pulled thread: A weaving technique manipulating the warp strings with a row of weft and leaving the warp visible.

roving: An unspun material before the yarn stage.

rya: A weaving technique to create fringe.

sapma: A supplementary weft technique using two tails that cross within the shed.

selvedge: The edges of the tapestry, marked by the last warp yarns.

sett: Number of warp strings per inch.

shed: The open space created when the warp is separated to allow the weft to be guided through.

shot: One row of weft.

shuttle: Device to guide the weft through the warp; can be a needle or pick-up stick.

soumak: A weaving technique that wraps the weft around the warp in a braid-like effect.

Spanish lace: A weaving technique creating small shapes within a single row of weft.

straight split: The edges of two shapes that end on parallel warp strings and butt up but do not connect.

supplementary weft: A weaving technique using a foundational tabby weft as well as a floating weft to create patterns and shapes.

tabby/plain weave: The weft travels over and under the warp evenly without any floats. Can be weft dominant or warp dominant.

tails: End pieces of yarn.

tapestry weaving: Freestyle weaving done with your fingers.

tapestry/panel/weave/wall hanging: Finished product produced from combining weft and warp yarn on a frame loom.

tassel head: The top part of a tassel that looks like a knot and is the part that you attach to a tapestry.

tassel neck: The middle part of a tassel with material tied around the bundle of yarn to hold it in place.

tassel skirt: The bottom part of a tassel where the bundle of yarn is cut into fringe.

template: Using a predrawn design as reference for weaving.

tension: The push and pull of weft versus warp.

triangle: A shape with three sides.

twill: An unbalanced weaving technique where floating tabby rows create patterns.

twining header: Woven at the beginning of a tapestry to keep the warp evenly spaced to its full width and hold the following weaves in place.

twisted floaters: A weaving technique where the weft during a tabby row floats and twists.

varied loops: A weaving technique after a row of tabby to pull out bumps of the material between warp strings.

warp: The vertical strings in a tapestry, held taut on a loom during weaving.

warp dominant: When you see more warp because it is emphasized by the spacing of rows or thickness of material.

warp string / warp thread: A spun fiber material that is strong, durable, and smooth. Usually cotton.

weave: Technique in which warp and weft yarns intersect while being held taut on a loom to create a packed panel.

weaver's knot: The best method to securely combine two ends of yarn of the same color so that they are invisible among the weave.

weft: The horizontal strings in a tapestry, which move through the shed with tapestries and shuttles.

weft dominant: When you see more weft because it is emphasized by the spacing of rows or thickness of material.

wool top: Roving.

yarn/thread/string: Materials used in weaving.

Acknowledgments

The timing for this book couldn't have been better for the people and events that surrounded my life. Thank you to my dear husband, Spencer Campbell, for cheering me on and pushing me to give all my best effort. Thank you to my mom, Tiffany Coulson, for the enthusiastic support, visits, and hours of phone calls as she listened to my anecdotes from across the country. Thank you to my editor, Sandra Korinchak, for reaching out and patiently guiding me through the process. Thank you to my marketing director, Jamie Elfrank, for the positive approach to every situation. Thank you to Emma Natter for creating beautiful custom styling boards for my photos. Thank you to all my mentors who have each taught me something that I needed to learn in the different chapters of my life.

hello hydrangea

Lindsey Campbell is the artist and instructor behind Hello Hydrangea. She has taught thousands of students how to weave through her online weaving video classes. Her work has been seen in Anthropologie, Nordstrom, Jo-Ann Fabric and Craft, Design*Sponge, *Simply Homemade Magazine*, and the *Huffington Post*. Lindsey lives in California with her husband, son, and their miniature schnauzer. You can find her at www.hellohydrangea.com.